STRONGER

You can Overcome and Bounce Back from Adversity

A 7 STEP GUIDE TO HEAL FROM WITHIN

Roula Selinas

BALBOA
PRESS

A DIVISION OF HAY HOUSE

Balboa Press books may be ordered through booksellers or by contacting:

Balboa Press
A Division of Hay House
1663 Liberty Drive
Bloomington, IN 47403
www.balboapress.com
1 (877) 407-4847

Because of the dynamic nature of the Internet, any web addresses or links contained in this book may have changed since publication and may no longer be valid. The views expressed in this work are solely those of the author and do not necessarily reflect the views of the publisher, and the publisher hereby disclaims any responsibility for them.

The author of this book does not dispense medical advice or prescribe the use of any technique as a form of treatment for physical, emotional, or medical problems without the advice of a physician, either directly or indirectly. The intent of the author is only to offer information of a general nature to help you in your quest for emotional and spiritual well-being. In the event you use any of the information in this book for yourself, which is your constitutional right, the author and the publisher assume no responsibility for your actions.

Any people depicted in stock imagery provided by Thinkstock are models, and such images are being used for illustrative purposes only.
Certain stock imagery © Thinkstock.

Print information available on the last page.

ISBN: 978-1-4525-3020-8 (sc)
ISBN: 978-1-4525-3021-5 (e)

Balboa Press rev. date: 08/19/2015

CONTENTS

Introduction ix

My Story...xi

Chapter 1   The Power Of The Mind 1
            Law of attraction. Affirmations. Visualisations.
            Attitude. Law of forgiveness. Self-care.

Chapter 2   Awakening Your Power..22
            Meditation, Connection. Be guided by how you feel.
            Mind Body Spirit – The Power of 3. Getting in touch
            with yourself. Reprogramming your computer.

Chapter 3   Faith..41
            Letting go of worry and fear. Intuition. Security
            guard at the door of your mind. Peace and harmony.

Chapter 4   Asking 58
            Surrender. Law of karma. Goals. Law of gratitude.
            Law of giving.

Chapter 5   Aligning And Receiving 71
            Love and deserving. Mind/Ego/Personality.
            Conditioning negative patterns to positive patterns.

Chapter 6   Getting Started..91
            Taking Action. Diet. Discipline. Exercise.
Chapter 7   Integration..101
            Balance. Patience. Persistence. Never stray off your
            path. Self-expression. Getting back to basics.

Resources 115
Acknowledgements...117
Overview..119

Dedicated to Mum and Dad my rocks,
and to my girls Danielle and Christina.

INTRODUCTION

You now hold in your hands a book that can change your life, if you allow it. This book contains the fundamental principles we need to apply to our lives in order to heal ourselves from adversity, to bring into our lives that which we desire, and maintain optimum health and wellbeing.

The Phoenix is a mythological bird that is said to live for about 500 years. When its life was up, it would build itself a nest that would catch on fire when ignited by the sun and burn and die. A new phoenix would then rise from the ashes to live again. It is a story of rebirth, immortality and resurrection.

In the midst of your darkest despair there is treasure to be found if you look within. In the darkness, a light can shine on the chest of gold buried deep inside you. If you search, these treasures can be used not only to heal ourselves, but to heal and benefit others, too.

I hope my story inspires you to not just overcome any challenges you are facing, but to rise above them and soar to even greater heights. I hope my story enables you to heal, to become stronger, more powerful and more whole.

MY STORY

I called my doctor early on the morning of 18th April 2007 to book an appointment in order to receive my blood test results – only to find that she had already made my appointment for 9am. That was strange, I thought, trying to stop my mind from racing as I got myself ready. With a feeling of dread welling up in my stomach, I felt sick as I drove to the medical centre. If they were to tell me there was nothing wrong with me, I knew I would have to get another opinion. Something hadn't been right for quite some time. I had been extremely exhausted and fatigued for the previous six months, far more than normal. The small lumps on my stomach, I discovered a couple of weeks earlier were unusual and had pushed me to finally get the blood test I had been postponing for ages. Everything seemed so hard now. Even just going on my daily walks or bike rides was difficult. Everything was such an effort! But, I just passed it off as exhaustion. Everyone gets tired, I thought, as I'd tried to dismiss it and get on with my life.

But I knew there was something wrong. I must have a virus, or maybe I had glandular fever. My stomach was in knots and I realised I was holding my breath, so I started to take some deep breaths to calm myself. 'Just take a seat, the doctor won't be long,' the receptionist said. Grabbing a few magazines, I sat down and flicked nervously through the pages.

After what seemed like an eternity, the doctor called me into her office. I sat down on the hard black vinyl chair as we exchanged pleasantries. 'How have you been feeling?' she questioned me, looking concerned.

'I've been really tired,' I answered, shifting uncomfortably.

'We got the results back from the blood test yesterday.' The doctor paused and looked at me.

'How were they?' I asked.

'Have you been sick lately?'

'No, just exhausted all the time,' I answered.

She nodded her head sympathetically before continuing, 'I'm really sorry, Roula. The blood tests show you have either leukaemia or lymphoma.' I sat in stunned silence. I must have heard wrong, I thought to myself.

The doctor proceeded to explain my white cells and blast cells were abnormally high. 'No, there must be a mistake!' I protested feeling nauseous. 'I probably have some virus—aren't your white cells higher when you have a virus?' Nodding, she cleared her throat. 'Yes, they are, but I am really sorry,' she said again calmly. 'We have a bed for you at the Royal Brisbane Hospital. You will have to go today so they can do some tests tomorrow. But you need to go today and stay overnight.'

All I could blurt out was, 'But my husband is at work and I have to pick the kids up from school.' Hoping for a reprieve, I asked anxiously, 'Can we go tonight after I pick the them up and he comes home from work?'

She replied, 'That's fine, but you must go tonight. We have a bed waiting for you, you cannot leave it till tomorrow.'

Having mumbled my agreement and thanks, I walked to my car, my legs shaking as if they would collapse under me. I drove home trying to concentrate on the road and not on what the doctor had said, but all I could think about what was I had just heard. My mind was going in circles. My body was numb. I hadn't said much at the doctor's office. This was not what I was expecting to hear. I thought I had a virus—but nothing like this.

As soon as I got home, I rang my husband Phil and blurted out what the doctor had just told me. As the words came out of my mouth, the reality that this could even be a possibility hit me, and the tears welled up in my eyes. Phil reassured me that everything would be all right and the tests would be fine. We were both secretly hoping it was a mistake and the tests would reveal that I did simply have a virus. My next task was to phone my dad in Sydney, but, with my mind in turmoil, I couldn't bring myself to reveal what the doctor had mentioned. I told dad they found something in my blood test results and I had to go to the hospital in Brisbane that night so they could do some tests the next day. 'I'll keep you posted,' I said to him.

To try to think of something else, I began some work that I had to do for my bookkeeping, but I couldn't focus for long. I then rang my friend Vicky who started to cry as soon as I told her, and then so did I. But, after that, it would be a very long time before I cried again.

With so many thoughts tumbling incessantly in my head, I finally decided there was no point thinking about it until I had been tested and I was told the final results. So I struggled through the rest of my work and kept myself busy with other chores until it was time to pick my daughters up from school. Giving them a simple explanation about my need to go to hospital took more courage than I thought I had, as I tried not to look alarmed or concerned.

I packed my bag and waited for my husband to come home from work so we could all drive from our home on the Gold Coast to Brisbane. When it was time for them to leave me for the night, it was strange to say goodbye and watch them go home. My youngest daughter, Christina, held onto me so tightly, tears streaming down her beautiful cheeks, begging me to come home with them.

We would be separated for a very long time, for we had embarked upon a very long and testing emotional and physical roller coaster. This was also the beginning of the end of my marriage. The next day's tests revealed that I had leukaemia.

I never expected anything like this could ever happen to me. I had exercised throughout my life and had eaten well most of the time. I enjoyed healthy food, drank my freshly squeezed fruit juices and took my vitamins. I had practised meditation on and off throughout the years, had tried alternative medicine and had taken my herbal remedies. I had a reasonably good knowledge of health and nutrition. Up to that point, I had only been sick with occasional colds and headaches. My doctors had previously told me on several occasions that I was one of their favourite patients: everything was perfect. According to them, I was textbook healthy.

Now I was faced with acute lymphoblastic leukaemia. Without treatment I had from a few weeks to a few months to live. Even with treatment, there was no guarantee that I would go into remission.

Having been physically strong and healthy throughout my life, the doctors assured me, would help me to endure the treatment I was about to undergo: chemotherapy, and then later a bone marrow transplant. I had never entertained the possibility of becoming so sick, and now, in the quiet of my empty hospital room, the doctor's words of diagnosis echoed loudly, over and over, in my mind.

Before my journey with cancer, treatment, surgeries and complications, my life had involved comparatively little struggle. I was born in King George V Hospital in Sydney, and for the first year of my life my family and I lived in Dulwich Hill. Then we moved to Wagga Wagga, a little country town in New South Wales, where my parents and some family friends bought a fish and chips shop. When I was about three, my parents moved to the inner-Sydney suburb of Haberfield where they managed a milk bar business. It was the local hangout for kids, with pinball machines, space invader games, food, essential grocery items and sweets. I was the envy of many of my school friends, as I had free access to all the lollies, ice cream and chocolates we could desire. I did pull my weight, though. From a young age I helped my parents in the shop, serving customers and stocking shelves. Despite this, my parents were often still very busy with the milk bar, and my brothers and I were left to entertain ourselves a lot.

I had two brothers: John, with dark hair and green eyes, who was four years older and my idol, and Tony, who was blonde, blue-eyed, cherub-faced and seven years younger than me. At four months old, Tony caught a cold that developed into bacterial meningitis. I remember the terror of hearing that the doctors did not expect him to survive, and that even if he did, they believed he would be left with severe brain damage. To our joy, he survived, astounding the doctors, but also showed no signs of brain damage or side effects. Whether it was my parents' faith and prayers, or divine intervention, or a combination of the two, I don't know, but from that day I have believed that miracles do happen.

I grew up loving books and reading. I would visit the library and pick out my favourite books, before rushing home to dive into worlds of fantasy. Much of my childhood was also spent being very active: I loved riding my bike, going to the park to play games and dance for hours. I also rode my skateboard, played soccer, touch football and other games with my older brother and our neighbours.

My parents were hard-working immigrants from Greece, who spent seven days a week at the milk bar. Despite all our play outside, my upbringing as a girl was quite strict compared to today's standards—there was a different set of rules for the girls and the boys. I wasn't allowed to do as many things as my brothers. Even if other girls were doing what I wanted to do, it didn't faze my parents.

We grew up with a strong, close-knit family. Our Greek culture played a huge part in our lives: we had frequent get-togethers, celebrations and outings with relatives and family friends. We were taught the importance of showing respect to our elders, of respecting each other and ourselves. I cherish the unconditional love and support that we experienced. My parents' unwavering devotion to us taught me the true meaning of love. Mum believed life's greatest treasures are your children, far more valuable than material possessions, and she was always happy with her lot. My Dad was hard-working, loyal and very well respected. They made a success of their lives and taught me that working towards what you want, and having patience and persistence, pays off.

When I started kindergarten at the local public school in Haberfield, I couldn't speak English, as my Mum insisted on speaking Greek. I attended special English lessons. From there, I did well in school. I was an above-average student and went on to a selective high school for top students. I believe education is extremely important, although I don't believe how well you do at school determines your future. Some people are lucky and know what they want to do from a young age, others it takes a little longer. My parents moved to Brighton Le

Sands when I was 13, in my second year at high school. Because of the distance, I changed schools but I quickly lost interest and focus. It wasn't until I was 25 years old that I developed a love of learning again. I began studying business management, bookkeeping and accounts, and personal development. Despite what struggles you may have to overcome, the best thing to do is to find what you love, have a goal, and work towards it.

We lived in Brighton Le Sands until I met and married my husband at the tender age of 20. I was a very quiet and shy child, and an insecure teenager, although I had the appearance of being quite confident. I carried a lot of fear within me. This was due in part to my personal make-up, my mother's fears and my upbringing. Since having battled with my illness over and over again, I have learned to manage this paralyzing sense of fear. However, we don't need to learn our lessons the hard way if we can avoid it, and I sincerely hope you can learn from mine.

What a different world I experienced during my time of illness and treatment! The nurses, doctors and staff at the hospitals were wonderful, and brilliant in every aspect of their care. It opened my eyes to a world I had never seen: a compassionate world where other people, even people who don't know each other, really do care about one another and want to help each other. It is very easy, in these days of readily available media, to focus on the negative things happening in the world. Fortunately, situations like this can bring out the best in people and I experienced that firsthand. Friends, families and strangers all offered their love, prayers, support and encouragement, as I was in and out of hospital.

In Australia we are blessed to live in a country with so much help available. Our public health system gives us access to world-class treatment. I am forever grateful to all the doctors and nurses at both the Princess Alexandra and the Royal Brisbane & Women's hospitals—they are outstanding. People from as far north as Townsville to as far south as Lismore in New South Wales came to the hospitals in Brisbane. The Leukaemia Foundation was amazing and I will always be extremely grateful for the help that they provided to my Mum and me while I was in Brisbane, away from my family.

My Mum and Dad moved up from Sydney for over one year to help us. Mum stayed with me in Brisbane while my father stayed with my husband and two children to help take over my role and look after the children (Danielle, then aged 11, and Christina, then aged 4) and the house. My husband, Phil, had just started a new business on the Gold Coast. There was not a lot of income yet, so, financially, it was a difficult time. Phil initially wanted all of us to move up to Brisbane. However, due to Phil's business and the kids' schooling, we thought this would be the best and easiest option for the family. But even the easiest option was hard for all of us to go through, but we dealt with it as best we could at the time.

My treatment at first was six months of one of the most intensive chemotherapy sessions available at the Princess Alexandra Hospital. I stayed in hospital for a whole week at a time (often longer, if there were complications), and the Leukaemia Foundation provided accommodation opposite the hospital for Mum and me. During these weeks, I visited the hospital daily for checkups and appointments.

I quickly went into remission; I was responding well to the treatment. I then had to prepare to undergo a bone marrow transplant at the Royal Brisbane Hospital. The doctors tried to prepare me as well as they could, warning me that I was in for a hard time. 'How much harder could it be!' I thought to myself, alarmed. What I had gone through was hard enough. All I wanted to do was run away and hide and not deal with anything else. If I could have found a rock and hidden under it, I would have done so. I was petrified and just wanted my life back. However, I knew I didn't have much of a chance without the transplant, as I had developed Philadelphia A positive chromium, which meant the leukaemia was likely to return. Without the transplant, I had 5% chance of survival, whereas with the bone marrow transplant I had a 60% chance.

For months we couldn't find a donor. My family and relatives were not a match, and to make matters worse, there were no matches in Australia. After a worldwide search, we found one match in the USA, but it fell through so I was back to square one. Without this donor, my chances were slim to none. I had to continue to stay positive and let go of everything, and again trust in the Universe to provide. I underwent two more chemotherapy treatments to stay in remission and ended up experiencing nerve damage in my feet. After another couple of months, a donor was found. They were from Germany, but they were only 80% compatible (a good match is 100%). Still, this was wonderful news, and it was my best chance for survival.

The stem cell transplant was to be done at the Royal Brisbane Hospital in Brisbane. The Leukaemia Foundation found my mum and me accommodation at the ESA Village in Brisbane not far from the hospital. Their brilliant services also included courtesy transport to and from hospital—this was extremely important, as the treatment makes movement difficult due to weakness, tiredness, sickness and extreme pain. This time, the chemotherapy was a much higher dose, though it was shorter in duration. However, its effects were even more intensive when combined with the high dose of whole body radiation I underwent, and far more severe than the chemotherapy of the previous six months. This was a completely different ball game: this kind of treatment is designed to wipe out not only all your good and bad cells, but all your immunity as well. Your body's memory of disease is erased in order to prepare for the new cells.

The six months of gruesome treatment at Princess Alexandra was just a warm up for the nightmare that was about to follow. The severe four months of treatment for the bone marrow transplant was followed by three-to-four years of numerous complications and setbacks associated with the transplant. I spent these years in constant repair, in and out of the Royal Brisbane and Gold Coast hospitals. I had numerous complications, graft versus host disease, where cells from the new bone marrow began to attack the foreign cells of my body. At first this acute gvhd occurred in my skin, then in my stomach. This also meant my skin was very sensitive and I was at a much higher risk of developing skin cancer. I was sick from various infections and from a virus that damaged my left kidney. I had four eye operations, steroid-induced diabetes twice from the drugs I was taking, and my gall bladder was removed because of inflammation and pain. As my body became more and more run-down, I developed chronic fatigue. A bout of pneumonia led me very close to death, and my last rites prayer was even read by my local priest. During this time, my kidneys also shut down. The severity of my pneumonia also resulted in a small stroke (which, thankfully, caused no side-effects).

To be honest, with so many setbacks over those years, I've lost count of them. Many times I physically couldn't walk up the stairs as my muscles had deteriorated so much. I've climbed the mountain of recovery so many times only to fall flat on my back and have to start all over again. These setbacks are hard, especially when you're so close to recovery. It was difficult and tested me on every level. But, I eventually overcame the pneumonia and the other infections. The diabetes also resolved itself. The chronic fatigue also got better with time, after three-to-four years of rebuilding myself again, physically, mentally and emotionally. I have slowly strengthened my immune system again, and regained my energy and stamina. But I still have to be careful to avoid coming into contact with all vaccine-preventable diseases, as my immune memory was wiped.

They say what doesn't kill you makes you stronger.

1

The Power Of The Mind

Awaken the gladiator spirit within.

You are reading this book because things may not be the way you want them to be and you want them to change. Maybe you are faced with adversity, you are extremely stressed or anxious, you are facing health issues, or you simply want to have and maintain better health and wellbeing. Perhaps your life is not the way you dreamed it would be. Whatever problems, obstacles or challenges you face, using these steps can and will change your destiny. My aim is to inspire you to make a real difference in your life and to make the necessary changes so you can overcome adversity, live the life you want and sustain optimum health and wellbeing.

This book is based on my study of successful people over the past 20 years and what has worked for them, and from my own personal experience. The steps that we will go through are based on spiritual laws that have been used throughout the ages. What is based on truth stands and survives the test of time. The laws can be used for attaining health, wellbeing, wealth, happiness and abundance. These same laws are applied in order to bring anything you want into your life. The actions, disciplines, words, thoughts and beliefs will vary for each of the things you desire, but the principles are the same. We will go through each of the steps that have been used by everyone (in one form or another) who has achieved great success or overcome adversity in their lives.

What I will convey to you is my understanding of what I have learnt on my journey of unscrambling and putting back together the pieces of life's jigsaw puzzle. While these principles of a life of health and wellbeing are simple, they require constant commitment, discipline and perseverance.

If someone you know has made the best dish you have ever tried, you ask for the recipe. In making your own dish, you may add or omit a few herbs and spices to suit your personal taste, but for the most part, you stick to the recipe. If something works, there's little need to change it. In trying to achieve something, we find out how others have done it, and then we try to follow similar steps to get what we want.

I don't claim to have all the answers to wellbeing and happiness. We are all learning something new every single day. You may not agree with everything you read here, and that is all right. Some of the principles of creating the life you want may awaken new knowledge in you as you read. Then again, you may already know of some of the principles discussed in this book, but perhaps you don't practise them. I hope to encourage everyone to put these steps into action, and to open your eyes to new approaches that could make all the difference. Take from this book what feels true to you and use it in your life. No one can learn anything, if they are not open to learning and to change.

In our Universe there are basic laws that we must follow to attain health, wealth, happiness and all the things we want. These are the fundamental principles to attain and maintain optimum health in our mind, body and spirit and for manifesting anything you desire. These are the steps for overcoming adversity and healing yourself. I will share with you my experience and what I have learnt throughout my journey. However, it all starts with you. Unless you put these things into practice consistently, things won't change. If you are serious about making the necessary changes, make a decision right now to commit to these steps.

I, _____, decide to do all that it takes and never give up until I get there.

There are many names for the Universal Higher Power we will be referring to in this book: Infinite Intelligence, God, Universe, Theo, Buddha, Jehovah, Divine Spirit, Divine Intelligence, Allah. Please use whatever name you feel most comfortable with using – there is only one Power.

Daily we are bombarded with negativity from the media—bad news, tragedies and poverty. We are influenced by other people's actions, comments and their beliefs. We're influenced by what's in, what's out, what we should wear, how we should act, what we should believe, how we should look ... and so it goes on. With so many influential forces surrounding us, sometimes it is hard to hear ourselves.

Law of attraction

Logic will get you from A to B. Imagination will get you everywhere.
Albert Einstein

There aren't many things we can control in this world. One thing we can control, though, is our mind. We are either in charge of our mind or it is in charge of us. Our thoughts are powerful, and what we think about consistently, we become. What are you giving your attention and thoughts to? The law of attraction is one of the powerful laws of our Universe, one we must be aware of in order to achieve the things we want in our lives. Many of us now realise that our thoughts send out frequencies that attract things, people, events and circumstances into our lives. Like a magnet, we attract what we want to us. When we think negatively, that is what we attract to ourselves, either consciously or subconsciously. It works both ways. That's why it's extremely important to be aware of what we feel and what we are saying to ourselves.

What we feel (and what we think about what we feel) becomes our perception of the world. What we attract to ourselves in the external world is a match to the vibrations of our thoughts and feelings internally. So it's vital that we protect what goes on in our minds. Get rid of negative thoughts, and try to avoid or minimise contact with negative people and situations: we don't need it. There is enough negativity in this world—we must put positive thoughts into our minds. We need to surround ourselves with happy, positive, like-minded people, those who inspire us or feel good to be around and don't bring us down. Often, caring family, friends and relatives (as well-meaning as they are) allow their emotional involvement, fears and doubts to influence us. They mean well, but we must realise that is only their opinions and beliefs. If you seriously want to change, it starts here: manage your thoughts.

Sometimes, we can't get away from certain negative situations or people. Observe and be aware of their comments and beliefs, and accept that that is their belief. That is where they are at the moment. We can't change them, but we can change ourselves. Be mindful; be aware and observe what they are doing or saying and how they are reacting to us, or how we react to them. We need to be conscious of what we are thinking and what we are saying. What we constantly tell ourselves becomes our belief. We need to become aware and monitor not just our thoughts, but our words too, for they are as powerful.

Focus your thoughts on positive things, on things that are good in your life and focus on what you want to bring into your life. When there is something we truly want in our lives, if you desire to bring it in your life, make it a study and learn as much as possible about it. We can't just be half-hearted about things and then expect them to show up. When we desire to have, learn and attain something and that is all we can think about, eventually it will come to us. Observe life and be aware of everything. Don't go through life without a destination.

Watch what you say to yourself and to others, as this sends out powerful messages to the Universe and to other people. We may not even realise what we're saying and do it subconsciously, so our need of becoming aware is crucial if we want to change things. If we want different results we must try a new approach. We can learn to manage our thoughts, focus them on feeling good, and pause before reacting to negative circumstances, events or people. They are living their day-to-day lives, doing the best they can. So it's up to us to be responsible for our actions and reactions and to make ourselves feel good. We can manage our minds, thoughts and environment. We can bring peace and harmony into our lives. When we always wait for other people to make us feel good, we will be disappointed. Making ourselves feel good first is the best thing we can do.

We all have challenges to deal with and overcome. Everyone has adversities—the rich and the poor, the young and the old. Look around, there is always someone worse off at the present time. The only people who have no problems are those that are dead. It is up to us to find solutions to our obstacles and challenges. Life is a mixture of challenges and opportunities for all of us. It is a combination of happiness and sorrow, light and dark, good and bad, positive and negative. Everyone is going to have their cross to bear at some stage of their lives. To start our journey of finding better solutions, we need to ask better questions. Don't get stuck on 'Why did this happen to me?' Rather, ask, 'How can I learn from this? How can I be better? How can I overcome this?' We must challenge ourselves to become better. Don't take the easy road and ask for life to be easier. Things will change for us when we change.

We experience a spectrum of emotions at different stages of our lives, so we have to realise and embrace not only the times when the sun is shining and things are going well, but find the courage to learn to walk through the path of storms and hardship, and then learn to dance again after the storms and cyclones of life have hit. We must gain the strength to move forward and find meaning and hope again in life and all its possibilities. We must rebuild our beliefs and hopes that have been torn apart, and recreate new beliefs, new dreams and goals.

I now realise that whilst we must strive to maintain calm, harmony and alignment, and avoid conflict and reacting every single day, there are times, perhaps when we are stressed, exhausted or fearful, when we do react. There will be times when life sometimes hits us with a baseball bat and temporarily bowls us over. There will also be times when people are nasty, cruel and vicious in their judgments and attacks. The thing to remember is that we are human and we are all doing the best we can. If we do sometimes succumb to life's pressures, day-to-day issues and dramas, then that is the time that we need to manage our thoughts. That is when we are out of balance and have forgotten the magic and wonder of the Universe. We must remind ourselves as soon as possible that our main aim is to feel good. Then is the time to stop, to remember to bring ourselves back into alignment and connect with our higher source.

Unless we live on our own on a deserted island, with all our needs taken care of, with nothing to do but meditate all day and no-one or anything to take care of, how can we expect that life or circumstances sometimes won't get to us? Just as understanding that 'happily ever after' is an unrealistic expectation and only exists in fairytales, life doesn't always go to plan. Sometimes our lives have huge obstacles to overcome. What we can do is manage our thoughts and make that a priority every day. If we do sometimes slip up, we mustn't be so hard on ourselves; we need to get back to feeling good again as quickly as we can. We are all busy with the demands of our careers or our home lives (raising kids, paying off mortgages or looking after everyone else and making an effort to work on our relationships). We are so busy that we have forgotten what we really want—after all, we all have the same basic needs. We have been so caught up with striving for more or working hard at our jobs to make a living and get ahead, but our core needs are the same.

It's easy to feel there are not enough hours in the day. As time-poor as we feel, we must make the time to connect back to ourselves and remember the wonder and Oneness of the Universe and of love. When we get lost in the day-to-day troubles, pressures of life, our personalities and misunderstandings, it is then that we feel separate. We are disconnected as our energy is scattered all over the place. When we recharge, regroup, refresh our minds and our spirits, we plug into the energy of the Universe and become whole, centred and balanced again. We must remember to come back to feeling good as quickly as we can. When we observe nature, we see there are periods of calm sunny days, followed by grey stormy weather; there is calm before and after a storm. The storms always come and go.

Just as the Universe has cycles and seasons, so we go through our own personal cycles and seasons. We have our springs as well as well as our autumns. We experience our summers as well as our winters. Some storms are more severe than others. Some people get hit by a hail storm, others by a cyclone or a tornado and everything gets wiped out. Our springs and summers are usually times of happiness—opportunities, success, creating the new, celebration and growth. Our autumns and winters are usually difficult times—challenges and obstacles, reflection and retreat. It's a time to make sense of the world and reassess our past experiences and our beliefs. It's a time to reflect on old thought patterns and beliefs and change them to new beliefs and new experiences. It's also time to take stock of where we are now and where we want to go. We need to reflect in order to learn from our success as well as from our mistakes. We must then set new goals, hopes, dreams and experiences for the future.

I am so grateful to all the doctors and nurses who helped me over the years. The doctors and nurses at both Princess Alexandra and Royal Brisbane hospitals, are second to none, providing world-class care. However, doctors and nurses can only do so much: it is up to us to stay positive, and manage our thoughts. They give their skill and knowledge so we can overcome illness. They are brilliant at what they do and they are essential in our society. However, it is our bodies that heal themselves. Focus your thoughts on good health; focus your thoughts on overcoming your challenges. Our bodies know how to heal themselves.

Most of us have heard of the placebo effect, where doctors give patients a sugar tablet or some other harmless treatment. They reassure the patient that this treatment has been used successfully for curing their disease. Once a user believes they are being treated, many ailments or illnesses can and do begin to correct itself and heal. This placebo effect is useful and effective, as it shows how powerful your mind and thoughts can be.

Listen to your doctors, but don't take what the doctors say as gospel. If you don't feel comfortable, get a second opinion and trust your gut instinct. A number of times I felt uncomfortable with what the doctors told me, I got a second opinion, and it proved to be right. Those times that I rushed in and just listened to them, I made a mistake. How many people have been told, 'I'm sorry there is nothing more we can do for you?' Those who refuse to believe this can be the ones who go on to succeed. They focus their thoughts on health and harmony, overcoming their obstacles and putting their energy into what they want to achieve. We are the ones who decide how and what we let ourselves think and feel. It may sometimes take all of our will power, however, we have to take responsibility for ourselves and our thoughts and beliefs.

Affirmations

Affirmations are a very important tool to help keep our minds on what we want to manifest in our world. Affirmations help keep our thoughts positive, and help keep our focus on what we want—not on what is happening in the current reality. To create our affirmations, we need to focus our thoughts on what we want to bring into our life experience and how we want to feel. Focus on what you want to be doing in the future—what you want to be doing physically, what you want your body to look like, and how you want to feel. Determine how you want your life to be and what you want to experience.

Now, write down exactly what you want to bring into your reality, in any area. It's important to state your affirmations in the now, make them specific and as if you already have what you want. Repeat them daily until the new thought becomes a belief. Once your new thought becomes a belief, your feelings will start to change about that subject. As your feelings change, your energy state will shift and things will begin to change. Repeat that affirmation until the time when you have aligned your vibration to match the very thing you want, and then in its own time, it will show up in your life. Below are some of the affirmations I have used on my journey to wholeness.

Affirmations

I am safe and protected.

I now have a healthy, strong body.

Things always work out for the best.

I have all that I need to heal my body.

I have perfect health and wellbeing.

I am strong and active.

My cells renew themselves daily.

I open up to receive the new.

I am now getting stronger every day.

All that I desire comes to me now.

My family is protected.

I open to receive my good now.

Abundance comes to me now.

My body is strong, active and full of energy.

My life is simple and easy.

My body knows how to heal itself.

I am strong and healthy.

I am strong, healthy and energetic.

I am grateful for all of the abundance in my life.

I have wonderful relationships in my life.

Wonderful opportunities come to me now.

Visualisation

If you can dream it, you can do it. Walt Disney

Visualisation is another important tool to use in conjunction with affirmations to change your negative thoughts to positive thoughts and to change your beliefs. We do this by picturing in our minds what it is that we want to bring into our lives. Imagine (with as much detail as possible) having the experiences you want to have. See and feel what it's like doing what you want or having what you want. With constant practice and repetition you will start experiencing less resistance (less doubt) and develop a stronger attraction (more belief), which will enable your energy to change. You'll feel better about that which you desire. Practise visualising what it is you want to bring into your life. Here are some examples:

If you want to feel healthy and have more energy
Imagine yourself doing your exercise (e.g. riding your bike) and feeling strong, healthy and energetic. Imagine the things you will see, feel and hear as you ride. It's important to use as much detail as you can. Visualise the scenery: the trees sway in the breeze, and you hear the rustle of their leaves; the grass is green, and you can smell it's just been freshly cut; children play in the park, and you feel the strength of those young bodies; you feel the wind on your face as you ride. Feel strong, healthy and energetic as you ride by.

If you want to feel more peaceful and be in harmony
Imagine yourself feeling peaceful, relaxed and in harmony with nature and your surroundings. You are in a garden or park it's a warm sunny day, the dog is running around and you are admiring the bird of paradise. Pause and admire the colours and shapes. Just like the flower, you are at one with nature, growing and thriving. Feel the wind in your hair, hear the birds chirping. Feel the peace. Your body—every cell—feels re-energised and renewed, and all is well.

If you want to feel more happiness
Imagine feeling happy and enjoying time with those you love, your family and friends, sharing food and good conversation. Hear laughter as everyone shares their stories and the food. Feel the joyful, relaxed atmosphere. Feel happy, grateful and blessed with all you have.

Our energy state attracts what we want to us. It's the way we feel about the thing we want that attracts it to us—when we can change our feeling to match the thing we want, then we are aligning with it and eventually it will come into our lives. We are in sync with what we want; we are on the same wavelength. Once we can get into the feeling and are able to sustain that feeling, that is when it will come to us. The Universe does its magic and orchestrates the people, information or the connections we need to bring us what we want. Meditation CDs or classes can teach you the visualisation process and help you get used to doing the techniques.

When I was having radiation treatment, I visualised a white light coming from the earth and into the soles of my feet, flowing all over every cell and organ and coming out at the top of my head and back down again like a fountain, over and over. I pictured this white light as healing my body, renewing and energising me. When I had chemotherapy I imagined that it was a white light going through all of my body, killing off all my bad cells and healing my body.

We can use these tools any time we choose to help balance, heal, realign and protect ourselves, and to bring about anything we want. The more we practise, the more our energy will shift. If we can hold on to that feeling of what we want, the stars will align and it will only be a matter of time before the thing we desire comes to us. Use as much detail as you can and practise what it feels like to have what you want in your life.

Words and thoughts send out vibrations; if we change our words and thoughts, we can change our destinies. We are only trapped when we feel powerless. The moment we realise and keep on remembering that it is we who hold the power to rule our world by our words, thoughts and feelings is the moment that we can start to change our world. The quicker we can change our thoughts to feel better, the better we will feel about ourselves—and, in turn, the better our lives will be. The Bible tells us that the truth shall set us free: you no longer need to keep the blindfold on. Take it off and let the light shine into every cell of your body. Know the truth and you will feel a sense of freedom. Practise and remember this so your world can change. Keep on repeating your new thoughts until they turn into beliefs. When you repeat the new thoughts enough, you will eventually start to believe them, and things will begin to change, and in time what you want will come into your life.

Attitude

When life gives you lemons, make lemonade. Dale Carnegie
It doesn't matter what happens to you, just what you do with what happens to you. W. Mitchell

When we become aware that we are responsible for many of the outcomes or events in our world and that we have created the circumstances or things in our lives, either subconsciously or consciously, we understand that we hold the key to determine our outcomes, and the power of the law of attraction. We realise why it is essential to monitor what we are thinking and what we are saying to ourselves and others. At times, things happen to us or to people close to us, which are beyond our control. However, when we realise that each person has a free will to create their own lives and make their own choices, we must all take responsibility for that and not play the victim. And we must also understand that sometimes life is unfair, unjust and cruel. Life has its ups and downs, happiness and challenges, and we need to look at the bigger picture. We must take responsibility for our own actions first as we all have a free will to create the lives we want. We all have a free will to determine how we react, overcome and what we take from these challenges. When we become aware that we are the creators of our lives by the decisions we make, the thoughts we think and the way we feel, we hold the power.

Your attitude to life and to the circumstances of your life can make or break you. Your decisions about the paths you choose determine your future and your outcomes. The people we associate with influence us; the opinions and beliefs of others that we allow into our lives can determine our thoughts and beliefs. Changing our words and our thoughts will help to change our attitude, which will change the way we feel. When we change our feelings about life, events or situations, we change the outcomes in our world. So let me ask you: what is your attitude? Are you a glass half-full or glass half-empty person? Do you look on the bright side or do you wallow in self-pity? Are you optimistic or do you play the victim? Monitor your attitude, and use your affirmations and visualisations to change your thoughts and feelings. Your attitude will change, and so will your destiny.

Two people can go through the same or similar event. One will sink into deep depression and stay that way, and the other will use it as an opportunity to learn and to grow. Once your attitude to life, and its events, changes from negative to positive, your life will begin to change. If you can see the situation in a different light, as a learning experience and one of growth or expansion, your attitude to life will change. Some things we can't explain: we don't know why or how some things happen, but they do, and we must accept that life sometimes throws us unexpected challenges. We must work out how to overcome them, and heal in order to rise above them. We can't overanalyse everything. Some things will remain a mystery. Look at the scheme of things in life and focus on the good stuff that is happening in your world, not the bad stuff. There is always someone worse off than you at this moment. It might sound simple in theory, but it's not always easy and it takes work and awareness and constant daily reminders. However, the more we practise changing our thoughts, the better we become at it and the quicker we are able to move on from a negative state to a positive state. Life responds to the way we feel: a positive attitude to life attracts and aligns to positivity. But what if you feel life is just too hard or painful right now and things are falling apart, and you just can't think of anything good at the moment? I suggest you find something good that is working in your life and focus on that and on how you want your life to be or what you want to bring into it.

Law of forgiveness

Whoever has no sin let him be the one to cast the first stone. John 8:7
Love looks forward, hate looks back, anxiety has eyes all over its head.
Mignon McLaughlin

We must learn to forgive others—and to forgive ourselves—for mistakes, faults and imperfections, and realise that nothing and no one is perfect. We must embrace our flaws and others' imperfections. Life is sometimes unfair and we won't be able to explain or work out why or how certain things happened. Things and events have happened to us, others have done the wrong thing to us, and we can't work out the reasons why we were treated that way. You've worked hard, been kind, caring and nice to people and people just walk all over you. Or all you are trying to do is get ahead and everyone else seems to be winning and getting all the breaks as your ust making ends meet. And why, then, has some unexpected misfortune or tragedy happened to you or someone you know? Life just doesn't seem fair!

These are the mysteries of life, the lessons for us to learn along our pathway. We must not let ourselves become angry or bitter – we can look at life from a different perspective, on a grander scale. We must learn to ask better questions. Instead of asking *why*, we must ask *how*. How can I learn from this? What lesson can I take from this situation and apply to my life, or use it to help others? Yes, sometimes life is unfair. However, we should surrender to the situation and leave it to the Universe, to the law of karma. Eventually others' sins, actions or hurtful words against us will come back to them in some way or some form, so we must learn to forgive. If we continue to do all the right things, the good will come to us.

Holding onto anger, hatred, resentment and worry only hurts us. Don't let regret or resentment steal your soul for it will chip away at the fibres of your being. You can feel bitter, or believe that life is unjust. Work on releasing your anger, resentment or bad feelings. Do whatever you need to do to let it out. Exercise, yell, scream, cry, talk to a friend, family, or a counselor. Write a letter or write in your journal, let the feelings out—just don't hold them in. Releasing these feelings is paramount to our health if we are to forgive, heal and move forward. We only hurt ourselves by holding onto them. We must let things go and turn them over to the Universe to handle. Even when people have done wrong by you or have treated you badly, set yourself free and forgive them and yourself for any mistakes. This is no easy task, but one we must work on. Maybe you wont ever understand or forget their actions, but do yourself a favor and forgive them.

Healing ourselves requires us to do the work, face our pain and loss, accept what is and work on forgiveness. It is a process, yet one that we must go through in order for us to freely move on and to cut all ties. Our job is to endeavour to make ourselves feel good every day and release any negative emotions, so we can heal, grow, have more joy and better experiences. Then we can experience peace, health, harmony, wellbeing and all the things we want. Remembering that others are at different stages of their journey, are struggling with their own demons, insecurities and battles, helps us forgive.

Techniques used for healing, peace or forgiveness:

- Meditation using breathing, concentrating on healing, peace or on forgiveness. Meditate on your own in a quiet spot for 15 minutes, or using visualisation CDS. Or you could find a quiet spot in your garden or in the park.
- Make sure you exercise. Walks in nature are a great example.
- Listen to music. This raises our energy levels, gets us in the moment and helps us let our feelings out while we are healing.
- Writing things down helps release pent-up feelings.
- Reading books.
- Find a hobby to help you focus on something else.
- Asking God for help.

- A support group of friends and family.
- Letting our feelings out is paramount in our healing. Find a support group that specialises in the type of healing you need, or you can talk to friends, family or a counsellor.

Research has shown that people facing cancer who had a strong emotional support network had a significantly higher chance of recovery.

Don't play the blame game when things don't work out the way you want. Many people blame others for life's shortcomings. They blame everything and everyone—their boss, the economy, their friends or their partners. They may blame their family or relatives, society or the government. Or they simply blame the sense that there is 'not enough time in the day'. We all have the same 24 hours to use to our advantage, to achieve what we want. Time waits for no one, so don't let it slip by. It's up to us how we use those 24 hours. Slow and steady wins the race, small steps daily, using our time responsibly and wisely.

We all make mistakes, but it's through taking responsibility and ownership of these mistakes that we can learn from them. Sometimes we don't realise that we're blaming others. We may be unaware of what we are thinking and saying to ourselves and to others. We may want something from someone, or a situation to eventuate, but because we are not getting it, we are resisting the person or thing we want. So we are unconsciously pushing away the very thing we want. That's the time we must ask ourselves if we're communicating effectively to ourselves or to them. We mustn't give our power away to others by asking them for their opinions on everything or letting their opinions affect us. We end up being influenced by them—and we ignore what we want or think—and then, many times we make mistakes. We must listen to ourselves; we must learn to listen to the still small voice within.

Sometimes when we want to change, we must limit time spent with negative people who have a bad or negative influence on us, or walk away from them. It is often the only way you can make the positive changes you need to. Sometimes we have to recognise that we have to cut ties with people that hold us down or constantly make us feel bad, because of their unrealistic expectations or their issues. Some people just can't forgive, let go or move past their issues. Some people have hurts and resentments that date back 10 or 20 years and they still hold onto them.

Some people are so rigid in their views and ideas, and believe their way is the only way. Some are so self-centred that everything revolves around them. Others play power games and try to control, manipulate or coerce you into doing things, or just take you for granted. Once we have realised we have done the best we can, it could be that cutting ties may be the best option in the long run. We can't change people, but we can change ourselves, forgive them and move on from their negativity and toxic patterns so that we can have peace, health and wellbeing.

Self-care
Love thyself Proverb

When we always try to please other people first, we are letting ourselves down. We cannot please everybody. If we are constantly trying to put everybody else's needs before ours, we will always be neglecting ourselves. We need to look after ourselves first, so we can be a better person for everyone else. Learn to please yourself, too, instead of always trying to please everyone first. We can't always say yes to everyone or everything; when we do, something in our lives will suffer, something will break down, something will give. Learn to say no. If you can't do something, or it doesn't suit you, it doesn't make you a bad person. If we don't look after ourselves, no one else will. Don't overdo things consistently and put ourselves on the back burner. We have to learn to put the life jacket on ourselves first in order for us to be able to help others.

Our body needs rest, recuperation and re-energising. Ask yourself what you want. What can you do for you? Do something that will re-energise you, so you can be in a better state to give to others. When we feel good about ourselves and our lives, it's easier to please and give to others. If we feel exhausted, stressed and empty, we cannot give of ourselves, because our energy tanks are low. We need to refuel, re-energise, refresh and reconnect to our Higher Power. Keep yourself feeling good by resting, meditating, exercising, or getting out in nature, or a doing a hobby that you like. How will you take care of your body, today? How will you take care of your mind? How will you take care of you?

Parenting is a most wonderful experience that teaches us many things. We get to experience life through our children's eyes again. It also teaches us many things about ourselves. The same can be said about work and all our relationships. We make mistakes, we have success, and we learn by these experiences. We must apply these lessons to our lives and use them to our advantage. Learn from observing your life and other people's lives, and you can apply these lessons to your life. Work out your strengths and your weaknesses and work on them. You need to take responsibility for your own choices, actions and words: sadly, many times we don't. No handbook can ever teach us how to handle every circumstance, problem or challenge we're likely to encounter. We learn as we go and we do the best we can. We must stop being so hard on ourselves.

We need to take stock and look at things more clearly and assess our past beliefs, actions and where we are now. If things are not where we want them to be, or we don't have our desired goal, we have to make changes. Clearly state your intention, what you want and how you want your life to be. Find out what the other person wants, or how we can be a better person for them, for when we give others what they want, we will get what we want in return. Sometimes we may not get what we want from some people, but we will get it eventually in another form from others. Treat people the way you want to be treated. If you want people to listen to you, listen to them, to their wants and needs. Learn to be a good listener. Remember what they want and like and try to give them what they want. We should make this a practice in all our relationships, in our work and in business. We have to find out what others want so we can get what we want in return. If we are not getting what we want or are unfulfilled in our jobs, careers, relationships, or desired goals, we need to see what we need to change.

If you want good health and wellbeing, take care of yourself on all levels (mind, body and spirit). If you don't like where your health, finances or relationships are at the moment, make new goals, set a new sail and adjust the course of your life. You are the driver and you direct your life where you want it to go. Are you steering a dinghy or a cruiser? If you don't like where you are at the moment, change it. We can't change others but we can change ourselves. We sometimes wander off our path, or take a different avenue. That's when we need to get back on our path to where we want to go. If things aren't working for you and you don't have the health, the relationship, the body, or the goals that you desire, try a different approach, or change things. Maybe your boss is taking advantage of you and you are unfulfilled. Do you have boundaries in place as to how much time you give or how you let people treat you? If not, then you need to set limits. Maybe you need to look at your relationships. Maybe you need to look at taking more time out. Or it maybe you need to learn more about what you want to achieve out of life, and how you want to be treated and what is acceptable to you. Treasure yourself and your worth, if you are not happy and fulfilled, find out what it is you really want and set about trying to achieve it.

Emotional wellbeing checklist:

- Are you fulfilled?
- Are your needs met?
- Are you working towards the goals you want and doing the actions required?
- Are you taking time out to rest and re-energise?
- Are you eating healthy wholesome foods to give you energy and feel good?
- Are you exercising?
- Are you taking time out to meditate or sit in quietude?
- Are you being mindful and practising awareness?
- Are you practising your new affirmations and visualisations?
- Are you practising new positive patterns?
- Are you remembering to focus on the good, not the bad?
- Do you have healthy, equal relationships, or are they one-sided?
- Do you have healthy boundaries in place?
- Are your boundaries respected or violated?
- Do you have healthy work relationships?

2

Awakening Your Power

Meditation & connection

The best and most beautiful things in life cannot be seen or even touched. They must be felt within the heart. Helen Keller

Life is hectic and demanding on all of us. We are all busy working, paying off mortgages, busy with our careers, raising our kids—or just keeping up with the demands of life!

It is important to learn to take time out and meditate for 15 to 20 minutes daily in order to connect to our Infinite Intelligence, and get in touch with the power that is inside each of us. Find a quiet place in the park, or somewhere private, if you work full time. Or you could find a quiet spot at home, anywhere that will allow you to quiet your mind and slow down to pause and take deep breaths to connect yourself to the quiet moment. When we quiet our minds, we allow our bodies to balance, restore themselves and rejuvenate our cells. We take time out from the constant chatter and thoughts in our own minds, and have a break from the demands what we are subjected to daily in our lives. Take advantage of the many good CDs or classes that can guide you through various meditation techniques. Focus your attention on your breathing, or pick a word ('peace' and 'relax' are favourites of many meditators) and repeat it over and over. Find what works for you, and then benefit from this daily discipline. When we practise meditation daily we learn to be compliant. In doing so, we balance and align, and we allow more of the good that we want to come into our lives.

Learn to make a habit of pleasing yourselves as well as others. As we explored earlier, there is nothing wrong with looking after yourselves. Take time out to do something that pleases you, whether it's meditation, sitting in a sunny spot, the exercise you like or a hobby you enjoy. If we don't make the time, we will never find the time because there are always things to do, other people to take care of, or deadlines to meet. We are responsible for making ourselves a priority and taking care of ourselves. Fill yourselves up, first, so you can then give to others. Don't always rely on others to make you feel good, because you will be let down: learn to make yourself feel good. By taking the time to quiet your mind, refresh and recharge yourself, and by changing the focus of your thoughts, beliefs and affirmations, you are aligning to your power. When we always rely on others to make us feel better, we are not standing in our power. Meditation allows us to connect to our Higher Power. Other activities which access our power and alter our moods are tai chi, yoga, karate, pilates or any exercise we enjoy: they help keep us centred, balanced and aligned as well as being a wonderful way to lift our mood and stay fit.

Taking time out for ourselves may be as simple as spending time in our garden, walking along the beach, going for a swim, going to the park, exercising or walking in a rainforest. As we do this, we are connecting to the universal energy and to nature. Perhaps now is the time to start doing things you've always wanted to do, but have put off. Find that outlet, that interest that you love to do and immerse yourself in it. We nourish our soul as we do this. As our lives are hectic and busy, we must take time out and give to ourselves so that we can give more to others. It's important to have a balance of work, rest and play in our lives. Our lives are demanding, but we need to make a little time to connect with our real selves and bring our body into alignment with our true power.

We are all students in this game of life. I believe no matter what our age, we can learn something new every day. We all learn from each experience and each other as we go through the cycles and stages of life, but we need to be ready to listen and to want to learn. We can't teach anybody anything if they don't listen or don't want to learn. Knowing something intellectually is very different from understanding something emotionally through life's experiences. When we know something emotionally, it is entrenched in our soul, it becomes part of our being, we change and grow on a soul level, and it becomes part of who we are. We can understand the essence of it. It's like an apprentice: they learn all they need to know in theory at college or university, but it's when they go out and work in the real world and put their knowledge to use and learn by their mistakes and successes that they become better and better. We need to learn, too, from the people who know a great deal, older people, or people through life's experience have wisdom. But there are also people who know a great deal in theory yet don't use their knowledge and apply it in their life. Knowledge unused is wasted. Applying what we know in our lives can benefit us and the people around us. Sometimes when we hear or read something, we know what to do. Many times though, it's not until later when we actually have these experiences that we learn and understand the true meaning. Remember the wisdom in the saying, 'The student is ready when the teacher appears.'

Be guided by how you feel

Your feelings are the indicator to let you know if your thoughts are on track and are working for you or against you. We are guided by our emotions: they are our gauge. If we feel good about a situation or someone, we are in alignment, we are on the right track. If we feel bad about a particular person or situation, we are out of alignment, we are off track. Write down or observe what you are thinking or saying to yourself about that particular person or subject, then change it to a thought that makes you feel better about that person or situation.

For example, if we have been diagnosed with a chronic or terminal illness, we must not focus on that, the now (on the illness or the current situation). We accept what is; however, we must focus our thoughts on the future (on health and how we want things to be). If we are feeling bad every time we think about our health or can't think about anything but what the doctors have told us, it's vital that we change what we are thinking and saying to ourselves. We have to choose thoughts that make us feel better about that situation.

This is where the positive affirmations will work in changing the way we feel about our health to a more positive, hopeful position. If we repeat the affirmations enough, in time the new thoughts will turn into beliefs and our body will respond, and in turn our feelings will change. Repetition works here; we must repeat the affirmations over and over. Once we believe, we will expect the thing we want to come. If we can sustain that feeling of belief and expectancy, at some stage the very thing we want will come into our life. As we look at every single area in our life and observe the way we feel about it, we'll know if we're on the right tack when we feel good about something or a situation.

When we feel bad about things, we need to change what we tell ourselves, so we can feel better about that subject, and start focusing on the things that we want to bring into our life experience. The Universe responds to our asking and our feelings: ask and you shall receive. We must focus on the things we desire most intensely. Saying yes to something you want aligns the forces of nature to bring this into your life. Again, we must repeat it over and over until it becomes a belief. It also works in bringing what we don't want if that's what we're focusing on. It works both ways, both positive and negative: that's why we have to focus on what we want, not on what we don't want.

We must understand that losing is as much a part of life as is winning. It is harder to accept loss and go through pain. But to be a good player in life, we have to realise we can't always win. We must be prepared to lose as well. Losing can teach us far more about life than winning. Through pain and heartache, grief and suffering, we experience the full spectrum of life – the duality of the Universe. Look to nature as your teacher and you will see the duality of all that is. Understanding this concept makes it easier to accept loss, so that when we go through adversity and heartache, we're able to bounce back more quickly and better than if we continued to feel sorry for ourselves. The challenge or curve balls life throws you is probably not something that you want or ever wished for—but it may lead you to insights and a deeper understanding, spiritual growth, and a destiny you could have never imagined.

We all want to feel good. We must remember constantly, from the moment we wake, that this is essential for our health and wellbeing. It will help bring what we want into our life quicker, because the better we feel, the more things work for us. It is our God-given right to feel good: we all deserve to have good health, happiness and abundance. If we can commit to a daily practice of these principles, we will be looking after ourselves and will have the peace, health and wellbeing we all crave and which is ours by divine right. For when we feel good about things, we are more likely to look after ourselves on all levels (mind, body and spirit) than when we don't feel good.

We can train ourselves to have better habits as we become more aware of what we are doing and saying. We can start by reprogramming our negative thoughts and replacing them with positive ones. We must identify what we want and what we don't want. We must realise that if we don't change, things will stay the same, or get even worse and disintegrate. Once we are aware of our thoughts and aware of what makes us feel good and bad, we must replace those bad-feeling thoughts with good-feeling thoughts.

Rule our thoughts and we rule our world. We can pay attention to and manage our habits and thoughts. We determine which thoughts we allow into our mind – no-one else can do that. We determine whether we take on board other people's cruel or vicious comments or behaviour. It's a reality that it's harder when our emotions are involved. By becoming aware of what we say to ourselves and how we are feeling, we soon realise if we have taken on board other people's negative comments or beliefs, or let situations get the better of us. Then we must release these feelings so we can move more quickly to a better feeling place. It is we who has to monitor and manage our reactions to others or negative situations. It is we who have the power to make ourselves feel good or bad. It is we who determine how long we will allow ourselves to go on feeling bad. When we are feeling bad, we must change what we are telling ourselves. And realise, even if we don't understand it, that it's the other person's belief or opinion, their insecurities, fears or issues, and that they are reacting. Focus your thoughts on things that make you feel better.

Here are some examples of the ways I've used these techniques to help me to change my thoughts and feel better:

- *Get active do some work that you need to catch up on, even gardening or clean out your cupboards or garage. I find it helps to distract me and put my focus on something else.*
- *Think of things that make you feel better.*

- *To release the negative thoughts into the Universe, imagine the thought leaving you and you are cleansed letting it float out to the Universe to handle. Breathe while you are visualising this and feel it leave you.*
- *Put on some music, change your focus and visualise things that make you feel better, or that you want.*
- *Imagine the scenario you do want and create good-feeling thoughts about the particular area you are concerned with or having trouble feeling positive about.*
- *Go to the beach or park, spend time in nature and release all your negative energy to the Universe and visualise it is taken away.*
- *Imagine a white light flowing up from the soles of your feet and out to the Universe like a fountain, cleansing you, washing away the negativity.*
- *Do any form of exercise to release good feeling endorphins and visualise what you want,*
- *Meditation or deep breathing to help you get back in alignment and concentrate on releasing your negativity. Or find a quiet spot in the park, or your house and spend 15 minute aligning.*
- *Write down or think of some new thoughts that will challenge the ones that make you feel bad and put them up where you can see them and repeat these new affirmations.*

When we are aware that we have good and bad thoughts, both positive and negative in us, we can accept our and other people's imperfections. When we slip into negative thoughts and patterns, we can get out of them quicker, simply because we're aware of them. We must not neglect to take out the weeds (all those negative things) in our mind gardens, otherwise they will run riot and be uncontrolled. We have to sow the plants we want to see in our garden: plant as many as we can, so there is no room for weeds. When the weeds do surface—as eventually they always find a way—we need to pull them out quickly, before they get too strong and overtake our gardens.

Our negative thoughts can be our worst enemies, for they determine how we feel, and the way we feel determines our reality. We must manage our negative thoughts (our demons) for they can hold us captive. Don't be your own worst enemy. Our thoughts can keep us tied and bound in chains, if we allow them to. Unlock the shackles and their hold on our mind and don't let them hold you prisoner.

We must constantly remind ourselves of the wonder and the mystery of this Universe and do our best to be in the present moment. We have to make a conscious effort to stop, enjoy the moment and notice the beauty, love and oneness, and appreciate how everything works and flows. When I forget and succumb to life's pressures and let stress overwhelm me, it is then I am more likely to react. It is then that we can get lost in our personality and feel the separateness, as no one else seems to understand what we are going through. When we only look after everyone else and prioritise other things and people before ourselves, we are not being kind or taking care of ourselves. We've moved out of the realm of beauty, love and oneness.

Many of the struggles we have are within ourselves; they are not on the external. Much of the turmoil we feel and the battles we have are within us. Life is not meant to be a struggle: we don't have to carry the whole burden and feel alone and struggle towards our goals and desires. Many of these struggles we have internally has a lot to do with our conditioning from an early age.

We don't have to feel we have to do it all each and every day. We need to pace ourselves, for tomorrow is another day. We need to ask, state our intentions (our goals), let go and have faith. Surrender our control and let the Universe take over to orchestrate all our desires to come to us. While we're expecting and believing that what we want will come to us and we're preparing for its arrival. We must state our intention and have a plan in place and work towards that plan. But first we need to let go and surrender our will and control and have faith. Sometimes things come to us in the most unexpected ways – we need to be awake to opportunity when it arrives. Let go and let God; trust in the process of life. Manage and challenge your enemies (negative thoughts) and replace them with positive thoughts, in doing so we are bringing what we want to us quicker.

Good-feeling thoughts.

- I am connected to the Universe and peace and harmony.
- The Universe provides for me and knows what's best.
- The Universe always looks after me.
- I am safe and protected.
- I have everything I need to do whatever I want.
- Abundance comes to me now.
- I am strong and healthy and full of energy.
- Feeling good is my priority.

Mind, Body, Spirit: the Power of 3

Three is the number of creation, the Holy Trinity the Father, Son and the Holy Spirit – three is a magic number.

Build your foundation on solid ground (faith) and even if it is blown apart by the cyclones and tornadoes of life, you will have the hope, faith, strength and courage to get up again, rebuild your life and start anew.

There is something to be said when you take a leap of faith into the unknown, it's as if something magical begins to happen. When you don't know how things will turn out but still fearfully take the first step—whether it's towards your goal, rebuilding your life or walking away from something or someone—or finding the courage to overcome the pain and loss and start anew. There is a magic to life that sets in motion when you follow your path. When you learn to listen to the voice within and trust your inner knowing and walk out into the jungle like a blind fool, not knowing how you are going to make ends meet, not knowing how you are going to start again, not having a clue how to rebuild your life or get to your desired goal. When you walk the path of your truth, life will eventually fall into place and orchestrate your desires to bring you what you want just like magic. Believe in life's magic for with the power of three we can do anything. With God all things are possible. Through God we are reborn again, we become stronger and we become more.

Keeping the mind, body and spirit in balance requires effort and concentration. It is important not only connect us to our Power, but also to refresh and re-energise us on our mental, physical and emotional levels. When we connect to our Higher Power, we are connecting with who we really are at our core, and our lives will be in harmony and balance. As we align with the Universe, we will have the ultimate gift of peace, health and wellbeing; we will have more energy and stamina. Happiness will be fleeting if we constantly rely on external sources to make us happy. We will have more happiness and fulfillment when we learn to look within.

We must take away as many stresses and external distractions that sidetrack us from connecting to our inner source of happiness and fulfillment. Our personalities reside in a time zone reality, so everything we do must fit into this time space, thus adding another pressure on top of the stresses of day-to-day issues. As we get rid of as many stresses we can and simplify our life, we connect to our own fountain of wellbeing. Live for the moment as much as possible, not in the past or future. Learn to live for today and let tomorrow take care of the future. Be careful what you wish for as it may not really be what you want, once you get it. Sometimes what we wish for may be different to what we think when we actually get it. Sometimes the dream is better in fantasy than in reality.

The more things we acquire, the more responsibility we have to look after and maintain them, the more tied we become to the things we own. We become the slave. Our commitment to these material things traps us; sadly the only way to learn this is when we have them. After all, we're not taking anything with us when we finally leave this life. It is wonderful to have luxuries and a comfortable lifestyle, but do we really need everything the marketers try to sell us? Simplifying our lives means less stress, less worry, and the less we have to work to pay for the upkeep of things. We are here to experience things and enjoy ourselves along the way. Everyone strives for a comfortable lifestyle, but we need to rethink how much we really need or want. We all have the same basic needs: to love, to be loved, to have our basic necessities covered, and to maintain peace, health and wellbeing.

Many times we think external things will make us happy, yet once we achieve them the happiness is short lived, and we begin to crave another new, external thing. The hole is bottomless. So connect to the fountain of internal fulfillment, by making the time to be in the moment as much as possible daily and connecting to our spring of Divine energy.

By managing our thoughts (mind), looking after our physical self (body), and uniting to our Divine Power (spirit), we are joining forces with the Universe. When we realise that we have both positive and negative, dark and light in us, we can let go of the unrealistic expectation that we must always be positive 100% of the time and that we will never slip up, get upset or react. We must always be conscious of the way we are feeling and strive to make it essential to feel good daily. We can manage our thoughts and emotions, so if we do forget and fall into the personality and our negative habits, we can quickly change our negative thinking and move back to a place of love, peace, harmony and balance—for that is us at our core.

The more we do this, the better we will be at it. We can move back to a better-feeling place faster, away from that place of not being aware and staying in the negative place and our personality. Move back to the present and remember the magic and wonder of the Universe. If the present is too painful to deal with right now, have hope and faith that you will overcome this and things will get better. Opportunity comes after difficulty, happiness follows pain, the sun always shines after storms, and a rainbow embraces the sky after rain, giving us the promise of hope. Things are temporary, time heals all wounds and scars, we may never forget but we can heal. As long as we move forward, learn our lessons and release our pain and our negativity. Then we grow and become more and whole again.

Getting in touch with yourself
Know thyself. (Socrates)

It is extremely important to know our strengths and weaknesses. We have to utilise our strengths and work on weaknesses. Listen and be aware to what we say to ourselves and to others. We need to constantly check our emotions and see where we are at, for our emotions are our guidelines. If we feel good we are on the right track, we are in alignment. If we feel bad we are off track, we are not in alignment, we are resisting. We need to move to a better-feeling emotion by changing our bad-feeling thoughts to good-feeling thoughts. We must learn not to fight and push (resist) against the current, when things don't go our way; or aren't turning out the way we want, or coming about in the time frame we want. It's when things aren't going our way that we tense up and become filled with anxiety and fear. Remember to let go and go with the flow; let the current take us where we are meant to be. As mentioned previously as we go through life, we go through a range of experiences, both positive and negative. As a result we also experience a range of emotions, from bliss to despair.

Even though we aim to be positive daily, we should remember because of the ups and downs and curve balls that life throw us, it is unrealistic to be 100% positive all day each and every day. We must remember the value of staying true to ourselves and letting life touch us so that we grow and evolve. When it's time to be happy, we should be happy; when we experience suffering and loss, we must allow ourselves the time to grieve. It's easy for others to say to move on, but we must first grieve, feel our pain, loss and suffering in order to fully be able to move into the new. It's only in facing and embracing these emotions that we can heal, grow and move past them. If we don't deal with our pain, losses or our issues—just burying everything deep down, they just lay dormant—only to resurface again and again. We are actually hurting ourselves by holding onto anger, resentment, pain and loss. These feelings don't just go away; we need to confront them head on. Allow yourself the time of grieving for we don't want to be stuck in anger or resentment and end up being bitter. If they are not dealt with, they stay locked in the vault which you thought you had forgotten about, yet they are there, simmering, only to rise up again and again. Survivors know they must face their pain, fears, issues or mistakes and learn from their lessons so they can move to a higher place, where they evolve and become more. As we become aware of our feelings and give ourselves the time and space to reflect, to feel the pain or loss, we can move past and release those feelings, and return to feeling good. The more quickly we can do this, the sooner we can reach that good feeling place again.

We must realise that our thoughts and patterns affect the way we feel and act, and contribute to our perceptions of the world, therefore influencing the way we react to people, situations and events, and determine how effective we are at bringing about what we desire. We must distance ourselves from as much negativity as we can and try to associate with positive people. Many people get stuck in their negative patterns, which can bring us down as they try to make us feel bad. They drain and suck the life out of our energy so they can make themselves feel more powerful. If we can become aware of this, and change the way we think, feel and react—know our weaknesses, strengths and flaws, we can change our patterns of thinking and feeling and reacting. And turn our negative patterns into positive patterns, which ultimately changes our moods, experiences and what we attract and our world.

Generally we act and react to different experiences and people based on our values. Our values play an extremely important part in our decisions, our emotions, our relationships and our lives. Our family conditioning plays a huge part in determining our morals and values. Understanding our emotions (which for the sake of these exercises I'll call good and bad feelings because that is exactly how we feel when we experience these emotions) helps us clarify our values. Of the many different words to describe an emotion, these are the basic ones.

Good emotions – ALIGNING

Bliss	Faith
Love	Trust
Happiness	Hope
Joy	Peace
Contentment	Harmony
Gratitude	Excitement
Appreciation	Calm
Satisfaction	Respect
Forgiveness	Confidence
Empathy	Appreciating, Valuing
Giving	Honesty
Wonder	Belief
Praise	Abundance
Secure	

Bad emotions – RESISTING

Grief	Regret
Blame	Anger
Dissatisfaction	Rage
Unappreciated	Hatred
Jealousy	Depression
Overwhelm	Resentment
Pressure	Unforgiving
Discontentment	Fear
Isolation, withdrawal	Worry
Dishonesty	Anxiety
Guilt	Insecurity
Jealousy	Disappointment
Greed	Stress
Disrespect	Criticising
Distrust	

If our values are constantly not met or violated, we may feel disrespected, unappreciated or unimportant as our self-esteem starts to diminish. Being aware of our feelings and values helps us clarify what we want, how we want to feel, how we want to be treated and what we are willing to put up with.

Reprogramming your computer

The illiterate of the 21ˢᵗ century will not be those who cannot read and write, but those who cannot learn, unlearn and relearn. Alvin Toffler *The son of man is come to seek and to save that which was lost.* Luke 19:10

We must be able to be flexible and work on changing our thoughts, beliefs and patterns. Accept what is and unlearn the old thoughts, beliefs and habits. In order to move into our new future we must avoid, and not repeat, our past mistakes or negative habits. It's crucial that we relearn new ways and not repeat the same way we used to do things.

For when life throws us its unexpected twists and turns that seem to come out of nowhere and turn our lives upside down, we must be adaptable to change. We may surprise ourselves and like our new lives far more than we ever imagined we could. But to get to this good place again we must do the work on ourselves and go through the process of healing.

When we are drowning in our sea of pain, we must find a life raft and cling to it. Use it as our anchor of hope to rescue and raise ourselves up from our depths of despair. We must remind ourselves daily of the feeling we're striving for, or the goal we want—every day until we reach that place. When we can identify what we are feeling, we can look at our beliefs about that particular situation or person. If they are good thoughts we are on the right track. If they are bad thoughts we are off track—and we need to change our thoughts and our beliefs.

Anchors to use for reprogramming our computer are:

- Affirmations, visualisations.
- Anything that we can use to remind us to be grateful every day.
- A picture or a memento of a time when we were happy.
- Sayings or pictures to put up in our house where they will remind us to be positive and have hope daily.
- Pictures or sayings of things that we want to achieve, placed where we can see them.
- Reading our written goals daily.
- Reading self-help, inspiring or educational books.
- Meditating; listening to personal development CDs.
- Exercise—get active if you can, if you can't exercise your mind.

- And (very importantly) deep breaths (remember to breathe) when we are stressed, fearful or upset we tend to take short breaths as we tense up.

Here's an example of how you can reprogram those negative thoughts to positive thoughts.

If you're feeling fearful or angry, write down what you are saying to yourself and change it to a better-feeling thought (in writing it down we become more aware of the negative thoughts and can create new ones that will challenge the old thoughts).

That's a simple technique we can all use; it's a way to put into practice the principles we learnt earlier.

You may be worried that something bad might happen to someone you love or you care about. Or you may be worried that a particular situation may not eventuate or come to you. You may have a lot of anger and resentment about someone who has hurt you.

We need to move from that space and release it, to find a way to forgive or to ask what we can learn from the situation. We change what we tell ourselves; we change the way we react to the situation or person. If we find it too difficult, ask God to help. (see Chapter (Law of Forgiveness) for techniques.

Bad thoughts
I'm worried that I don't know how we're going to make ends meet.
I'm scared that something bad might happen when my kids go out.
I'm worried that something bad might happen.
I feel that I won't ever find the job I want.
I'll exercise when I feel better.
I'll watch what I eat, starting tomorrow.
I'll start to exercise next week.

I don't think I will ever find the partner I want.
Everything is too hard.
Why do these things always happen to me?

Good thoughts
Things always work themselves out in the end.
The Universe always provides for me.
My family is safe and protected.
I am safe and protected.
God looks after me, I am safe.
My body is strong and healthy.
My body knows how to heal itself back to perfect health.
Today is the start of a bright new future.
I feel healthy, fit and strong.

Write any down any that may apply to you, or make up your own affirmations that are relevant to you and your situation. Repeat that thought over and over, every day. Eventually it will become a belief and you will start to feel better. In feeling better you are aligning with that energy and you will come to attract what you want into your life.

Affirmations
These affirmations are inspired by the work of Florence Scovel Shinn. I have found her affirmations powerful and used them throughout my life and recovery. Using my own words makes it resonate stronger with me. I recommend you rework my words to make it even more powerful for yourself, and make up some of your own.

God controls the situation.
Peace and harmony now fill every cell of my body.
Wonderful opportunities come to me now, in perfect ways.
God provides for me.
God protects me and I am safe.
Things always work out for my highest good.

I have wonderful relationships in my life.

I now have perfect health and harmony in my mind, body and affairs.

I now have perfect health and harmony in my mind body and spirit.

I release all guilt, fear, hurt and resentment.

I let go of all fear and trust in God.

I have peace, harmony and abundance. All is well.

All I want comes to me in perfect ways.

I am one with God, and all my good flows through me.

I turn my burdens over to God.

3

Faith

You are ushering in another day untouched and freshly new, so here I am to ask you God, if you'll renew me too. But Father I am well aware I can't make it on my own, so take my hand and hold it tight for I can't walk alone. Helen Steiner Rice

Not everything can be explained, some things have to be believed with faith.

There is something far greater out there—a Higher Power, a life force, a Divine intelligence. Although there are many names for this power, they are one and the same. We need to learn to have faith in the Universe and trust that everything will turn out all right in the end, and that there is a perfect order to this world; a perfect order based on love and wellbeing. We can't control all of the events and circumstances in our life, and we can't control other people. Some things are beyond our control, some things will remain a mystery.

Other things we won't ever be able to explain why or how they happened—they just do, and that is life. We can't control the weather or what happens in the world or what happens to the other people around us.

However, there is a Higher Power inherent in all of us and we can connect to this Supreme Power at any time. This Supreme Intelligence knows exactly how to make our bodies work and to make ourselves healthy or repair itself again, how to run this Universe and everything in it. Once we realise we are far more than our physical bodies, we must learn how to surrender our control and our desire to plan and control everything, and to develop faith and trust in the process of life and its wellbeing for all of us.

There is no security in this world: it doesn't matter what job or career you have, how much money you have, who the people are that you love, or how many material things you have acquired along the way. Everything can disappear in a matter of a few seconds. One accident, a mistake, a wrong decision can set us back or change our lives forever. The loss of a loved one or a job, bankruptcy, divorce, a tragedy or illness can turn our world upside down.

As I said earlier, there is nothing wrong with wanting to be comfortable and having the material things and experiences we want. However we must remember that real wealth and abundance reside in us. We can have all the money or all the material things we want, yet feel miserable, lonely and depressed. It's the way we feel about things that's the most important. As wonderful and enjoyable as they are, many of these things are over and above what we actually need, they are excess. The bigger house, the luxury car, the investment portfolio, and the career we've worked hard at or dreamed of. Though they are fabulous to attain, enjoy and experience, they are simply not enough to sustain long-term happiness.

Life's uncertainties and material things underline why we must concentrate first and foremost on having and maintaining health, wellbeing and being happy and peaceful in the now. Helping others and being of service to them in some way can make us feel wonderful. Being appreciated, loved and making a difference to someone makes us feel valued. Whether it's one person, a family, a few people, or a community, we feel good and we make a difference and it's something we can't buy.

The only real security we have is our faith. Everything can be gone in an instant, our jobs, our health, our partners, our money, or our loved ones. Your world can be turned upside down in a few seconds with no way or means about how you are going to make it through. Our security lies in having a rock-solid faith that we will overcome any obstacle placed in our pathway and that things will get better than they are right now. Our faith is our real security.

Work on your faith, rebuilding your trust, letting go of your pain and working out what you want. We don't need to worry how we are going to do it or how it's going to come about. We need to state our intention and let go (surrender) and let God do its magic. When we want something, our job is to ask the Universe for what we desire and to move (the ego) aside and let the Universe provide it for us. We don't need to work out all the plans and all the details.

We need to truly desire that thing (it must be a desire, not just a wish), to ask, to stop resisting and become aligned with it. Be open to insights and signs as to what we should do and how we can start on our path. Put a goal and a plan in action and start your action towards the desired intention. Practice getting into the feeling state, or visualise your desired goal. If we persist on this path eventually it will come into our life, in its own time. Remember to surrender and allow all that we want to come into our lives, to flow through us in order for us to receive it. We must learn to live in the now as much as we can as well as keep our focus on the desired outcome. Have hope and keep our dreams and goals alive.

Letting go of worry and fear
Why are you so afraid, ye of little faith? Mathew 8:26

I was a good worrier. I was good at worrying about everything. But I had to learn that we can't control everything and all of the events and circumstances in our lives. What we can control though are our thoughts and the way we react to events, people or circumstances. It's not what happens to us, it's what we do about it. All of us face life's challenges, obstacles and adversities: be it financial, health, career or relationship. It's up to us to rise to the challenges that confront us and work with the Universe to find solutions for them to be overcome or find ways to heal. In doing so, we grow and expand and become more.

You might think life is unfair, and sometimes it is. However, we need look at the bigger picture, there is always someone worse off than us at that time; someone who is doing it tougher and harder than us. If you think your life is bad, take a look at some people who have huge obstacles to overcome or who have faced unimaginable tragedies in their lives and have come out the other side with a smile on their face. Don't waste time thinking about regrets and mistakes. Regret can eat at our core like a virus if we don't tame the beast. Bad decisions, mistakes, accidents, adversities, people who have hurt us—don't let regret keep you stuck. Many things are thrown at us unexpectedly; they may not be what we want, but we must eventually accept them. Look for the lessons they are meant to teach us. That's when we need to open our eyes to the good we have in our life, and look at others in worse positions. We all make mistakes: this is how we learn. Don't spend wasted time worrying about tomorrow. Don't think about 'what ifs'. What if this happens or what if I had done this? It's easier said than done, yet we must move from that space in order to let go and heal. There's a great truth in sayings like: 'Think about today and let tomorrow take care of itself,' or, 'Live for today and plan for the future.' So let tomorrow come and let it unfold and try as best you can to enjoy the now. Don't be in such a rush to get to tomorrow, for tomorrow will come and you will wonder where the time has gone.

Worry, fear, and anxiety: they are nothing more than a lack of complete faith in a Higher Power. We lack trust in the process of the Universe and are worried that our plans won't eventuate or turn out the way we want them to, or come in the time frame we want. When life doesn't flow or things don't seem to be working, we resist, we fear, we worry and become anxious. That's the time we must put our faith in our Higher Power and let go and let God come into our lives.

As mentioned, if we run away from our fears and problems and don't deal with our issues, we are confronted with them again and again. It is only when we face them head on, and deal with our fears and our issues and stop resisting them that they fade away or subside.

All sickness is caused from a mind that is not at ease, one that is not at peace. Worry, fear, anxiety, anger, guilt, hatred and resentment: all are acidic thoughts and poison the blood. They damage our cells and cause stress and disharmony in our body and soul. Stress is toxic to our minds, bodies, organs and immune systems. To heal the body we must first heal our subconscious mind.

When you put enough pressure on something, eventually it will suffer wear and tear or disintegrate and break. This can happen in our bodies, minds, relationships and our health and wellbeing. Too much stress and pressure is not good for anything. When our bodies are under severe stress from poor diet or toxic thoughts or we are constantly under emotional stress things start disintegrating or breaking down.

When you hear someone say they feel sick when they think about something that is literally what is happening in their body when they think about that situation or person. We must look at our feelings, at what we think or say and at our actions and reactions. We then replace our bad (negative) thoughts and beliefs with good (positive) feeling thoughts. In extreme cases, after trying every option, we must decide whether it is healthy for us to continue to associate with those friends that bring us down, whether we stay in our jobs, or in a situation or relationship, and look at ceasing or severing ties. When we are aware of our thoughts and keep a constant check on them by the way we are feeling, it is easier for us to change our thoughts, feelings and habits.

Affirmations
These affirmations are inspired by a number of authors. I have used my own words to make it resonate stronger with me. I recommend you rework my words to make it even more powerful for yourself. All materials, quotes, affirmations and concepts I have used in this book or are referenced in the bibliography.

I am connected to Divine Intelligence and wellbeing.
I achieve all the things I want with ease
I have everything I need right now to heal myself.
My body now restores itself back to perfect health.
The Universe always provides for my family and me.
I now attract peace and harmony and things come to me easily.
My relationships are happy and harmonious.
Health and abundance are mine now.
I align with God and wellbeing.
My body is back to its perfect state.

Intuition

Be still and listen to the still small voice within. Proverb
The intuitive mind is where your genius resides. Artemis

Trust and have faith, there is a Higher Power that resides in all of us, but we must connect to it, awaken it and believe in it. Move the reasoning (logical) mind aside and develop your faith. Trust your gut instinct for it is never wrong; let it guide you in your life. Thomas Edison invented the long-lasting electric light bulb, radio phonograph and motion picture camera; Karl Franklin Benz invented the gasoline powered automobile. Both achieved great heights by trusting their intuition and following their leads, against all adversity, criticism and ridicule. Napoleon Hill's son was born deaf and mute but he vowed that his son would live a normal life and one day would be able to hear. When his son was a young adult he was given an opportunity to trial a hearing device. Now his son can not only hear and talk but leads a successful independent life.

Don't listen only to the outer voice of everyone else; learn to listen to your inner voice, for this inner voice holds the truth and is the truth. Most mistakes I have made came when I listened to others instead of trusting my instinct and listening to myself. Everything we have or do, we have attracted to ourselves, a lot of it subconsciously. We need to stop worry, fear, resentment and anxiety and allow faith and trust to be at the foremost in our mind. Things always seem to work out. Even when we are at our lowest, if we hang in there long enough and persist things always turn around for the better.

So it is our job to focus our attention on good-feeling thoughts, on peace, health, harmony, wealth and happiness. When we feel lack, we are attracting more lack into our life. When we feel abundant, we are aligning to more abundance. When we feel healthy and strong, we exercise more and take care of ourselves, we are attracting more of the same into our life. We attract that which we feel strongly about. It is a discipline, and we have to remind ourselves to do it daily, especially when we don't feel like it, or feel as if the world is tumbling down, and nothing seems to be going right.

When we can remember that to feel good is our daily main aim, we are practising happiness. For happiness and abundance are states of mind. We don't have to wait to achieve something to be happy – we can be happy right here, right now. Happiness is a feeling, and the thoughts we hold determine our focus and our state. We have to remind ourselves to focus on all the good we have, not on what we don't have. We don't need to rely on everyone else to make us happy: when we rely on others or better circumstances to make us happy, we give our power away and we may be waiting for a very long time. We can choose to feel more happiness by focusing on all the good we do have in our lives. We can make ourselves happier and feel better firstly by connecting to our selves (higher self), thinking better thoughts and taking the time to give to ourselves. Then we will start to feel better. Then we will stop resisting. Then we start connecting to our Higher Power. We re-energise, refresh, heal and balance our mind, body and spirit.

Life is wonderful, experiencing and sharing things with our loved ones, family and friends. Sometimes, it's time to make new friends, change jobs, get a new partner or set new goals, because we do constantly change and grow, and expand. But it is us who first choose to be happy – we can make ourselves feel happier by what we tell ourselves, and what we focus on. If we are not happy with where we are at right now, we must change things. We must remember to look on the internal not just the external. When we work out what makes us happy and what we are willing to put up with, or find out what we want to achieve, then we are practising awareness. When we become aware that we too play a major role and start relying on ourselves to make ourselves feel better first. Not just others or better circumstances, we will feel happier more of the time. When we feel happy we are aligning more happiness into our lives, and we will have more of these experiences. There still may be some times when you do feel upset, you do get angry and react. We can't expect to be positive 100% of each and every day especially while we are going through our tough times. However, when we are constantly aware of our feelings and thoughts, we will be able to move to a better-feeling thought and on to a good-feeling place far more quickly.

We constantly have new desires; they are never ending. But if we are constantly waiting to be happy only when we achieve money, our dream house, the body we want, or the relationships we want, we will never be happy for long. Happiness is a decision we make, and it is a choice, daily. Decide to be happy right now. You are at exactly the right place you are meant to be right now – even though you may not like where you are at this moment in time. If we don't like where we are at and want to change things, then we need to do something about it. Decide our new future. Decide what we do want in our life. Keep our spirits up and have hope. We change the way we see things and change our thought patterns. Remember to be grateful for what we do have, and—most importantly—listen to the voice of intuition within. Watch for sign or clues: they will point us in the right

Ask for help and wait for the answers to come to you: they will come in a variety of ways.

- *Trust your gut instinct, pay attention to your dreams.*
- *Really listen to the songs or things you hear on TV or radio—it may be exactly what you are meant to hear right now.*
- *Someone may point you in the right direction towards what you want to achieve, or that can help you in some way.*
- *Pay attention and be open to any insights or information you hear that strikes a chord—it may be just exactly what you need to learn, hear or act upon.*

- *Once you get an insight or a feeling start on your desired path—take action.*

Security guard at the door of your mind
Stand guard at the door of your mind. Jim Rohn

Protect what information from other people, society's beliefs and opinions you let enter your mind. Be aware that the information we put into our mind adds to our computer programming, which determines how we think, feel and act. Be mindful and watch how we react to people or circumstances. Don't let negative people or circumstances affect or upset you and steal your energy. We need a security guard at the door of our mind, to help us in our job of keeping ourselves feeling as good as possible all the time. When we get angry at certain people or circumstances, we are mostly upsetting ourselves. We only let ourselves down when we react to things that upset us. Remember our daily goal: to feel good. Remember what we've already learnt: change the voices in our head; think of ways to avoid getting upset or react and give our power away. When faced with obstacles, challenges or difficult people, think of better-feeling thoughts; challenge what we are currently thinking. Think of things that make us happy and change our focus.

We must manage our mind—otherwise it controls us and will run riot if not tamed. Just as a garden will be overtaken by weeds; unless it is constantly maintained so it is with our mind. Understand that people are at different stages in their life journey, they are reacting to their own struggles, issues and battles. It may be that we, unknowingly, are bringing up something that they are having trouble dealing with. Sometimes people throw stones at us, because we're awakening their own insecurities within themselves. They will never understand what you are going through unless they walk in your shoes, just as we must respect their journey. Sometimes we may need to disassociate or distance ourselves from negative situations or people in order for us to feel better, more positive and happier. When we change, avoid conflict and negativity, concentrate on feeling good, and stop resisting things, circumstances and people, life will respond differently. You will want to limit your contact with negative people and situations as much as possible for your wellbeing. Avoiding or running from our problems and not dealing with our issues is not the answer; we will be confronted with them again and again. It is only when we face them head on and deal with them and we stop resisting them that we can move past them.

Just as we put a security guard at the door of our mind. We must put a security guard around ourselves and how we allow ourselves to be treated. Boundaries are the way of the Bible. Boundaries are something we must enforce not only on our minds, but on our bodies as well as our emotional (spiritual) body (how we are treated). Do you find people respect or violate your boundaries? Just because we treat others nicely, and do everything for them does not mean we will get the same in return. Just because we bend over backwards for others does not mean we get treated this way. Some people take advantage of this nature and will walk all over you. Some people will want to bite the arm off that feeds them, never content wanting more and more. Others you give an inch and they take a mile. We must all serve each other, but not become a slave to others and forget about ourselves and put ourselves last. This is not the Bible way. God tells us to treasure ourselves. In having healthy boundaries in place on ourselves and what we are willing to give and by looking after us—we are respecting and treasuring our worth, as we set limits.

When people are controlling or violate your boundaries we do things out of fear or guilt and then we have anger and resentment. As mentioned we all must serve and be of service to others yet be respectful. In setting limits we don't or shouldn't have to come from a place of guilt, fear, pressure or resentment—but we should come

51

from a place of love and truth. If you find people are not treasuring your worth, are only looking out for themselves, expect more and more, only call or talk to you when they want something. If you find people are never satisfied or appreciate you and you only seem to be doing things for themselves. If you find people are controlling you with guilt, anger or fear. Then you need to ask yourself whether that relationship, job or partnership is one that your needs are being met and if you are fulfilled. You need to ask yourself whether this is a healthy two sided relationship or is it one sided. Is it a healthy equal relationship, job or friendship or is it unequal? And look at whether we have healthy boundaries in place. If not, then we need to look at changing ourselves.

Peace and harmony

Those things I have spoken to you, that in me you may have peace. In the world you will have tribulations, but be of good cheer, I have overcome this world. John 17:33

When we create a peaceful mind, we create harmony in our mind, body and spirit. Our mental, physical and emotional states reflect that peace and harmony. All our organs will function better, we will have more energy and we will feel good. All mental thoughts have vibrations; we attract what we vibrate to. Be aware and keep a constant check on what our thoughts are attracting into our experience.

While we all know that a balanced diet and exercise are extremely important, we also must have a balanced mind, a mind that is free from or limited by negative thoughts. Worry, anxiety, guilt, fear, anger and resentment are acidic thoughts that destroy our bodies: they are like poison. Toxic thoughts create a toxic reaction, which causes stress and damage in our bodies, minds, cells and immune systems. A body constantly under stress starts to break down and can damage our organs, immune systems or cells. Not only are we are doing ourselves an injustice, but we are hurting ourselves.

Daily reminding ourselves that the most important thing is for us to feel good and be in the moment as much as we can will bring more peace and harmony in our lives. By changing the negative voices in our mind, avoiding negative situations and conflict, we are aligning to peace and harmony and we are in sync with all that is good. Our body, mind and world will reflect the peace and wellbeing that come as we unite to our higher selves and align to peace and wellbeing.

It is our job to find solutions to our problems and obstacles; we must challenge the negative thoughts with positive thoughts. As mentioned we shouldn't have to struggle to get the things we want. When we reach the vibration (the feeling) of that which we desire, it is then that it is drawn to us. When we feel happy, we are aligned to that and more happiness will come to us. When we feel peaceful, our mind and body are at ease and in harmony and we have more peace in our lives. When we feel good about our body, we watch what we eat and we take care of it. Our body is in balance and in alignment and has more energy and vitality. When we feel healthy we attract more health and physical activity into our lives and we tend to watch what we eat even more. Our cells, organs and immune systems all respond to our feelings and our energy state. Peace and harmony start in the mind.

All things come to us as gifts. With the realisation of health we receive the gift of health; with the realisation of happiness we receive the gift of happiness. When we feel successful, we are given more success. When we feel abundant, we are given more abundance. When we are balanced we feel peaceful and calm as we align and receive the gift of peace. These are gifts that we must open ourselves to receive. When we are grateful for all the good we do have, we notice it more in our life because we are focusing on the good. But what if you say there is nothing good in my life? There's sure to be something you've overlooked and taken for granted, things that other people would give their right arm or their life for. Focus using the eyes you have that let you see. What about your health, your relationships, the roof over your head, or your job? Ask someone who has just lost their loved one what they would give to get them back. Ask someone who is dying what they would give to get their health back. Does the big mansion really matter anymore when you are facing death or you've lost your loved one? There is plenty to be grateful for if we just focus on what we do have and take for granted, because it's already here. It's helpful to put reminders up in our house, on our wall or near our bed, reminders of all we do have to be grateful for. Focus on the good—those things we sometimes forget we have and just take for granted.

We are so blessed, yet when things go wrong, we forget all the good and focus on all the bad. Yet we must recognise that we have these gifts and be grateful for them, not just take them for granted. We are given these things as gifts—because that is exactly what they are. It is our divine right to feel happy, peaceful, abundant and healthy. But we must open ourselves to feel these things and receive these gifts.

There is far more to wealth than having money. Is money enough if you have ill health, or even worse, are facing terminal illness? There's not anything like a wake -up call like that, to put things in perspective. Likewise is money enough to make you happy if you are always in constant pain, feel depressed, miserable, unhappy and lonely? Our health and wellbeing is number one, and is above everything else. What is the point if you are too sick or won't be around to enjoy your riches, or have no one you love to share it with? Having wealth can mean different things to different people. Being wealthy is not just about financial achievement: it's also about having our health, having people that love us, having friends and family to share experiences with, and enjoying what we do. We are all wealthy – once we realise it's the way we look at things, it's our perceptions of wealth, happiness and abundance that make the difference. It's about being grateful and happy for what we do have and what is working in our life: that, I believe, is real success and happiness. When we focus on all the good we do enjoy, when we are happy with what we possess, then we feel the abundance that makes all the difference.

For what advantage is it to a man if he gains the whole world, and loses himself or is cast away? Luke 9:25

While we continue to do these things consistently, we will have more peace and harmony and attract more of what we want to manifest in lives. Keeping this balance is crucial because success and the achievement of our goals can sometimes be different to what we expect them to be. The happiness and satisfaction of the achievement of goals are short lived; it's not long before we desire something new. Remember, instead of always looking at the external to make us happy, we should look to the internal for fulfillment. On our own we are one, we are separate—an unpolished raw diamond. Yet when we align to our Higher Power we become one with not only the current and the waters of life, but one with the entire Universe and with everything there is. We become more, we're on our way to becoming polished. We can never match the Supreme Power on our own, by connecting to it we align with it, we can achieve far more.

Why do most of us need to accumulate so many things? We seem to think that 'things' will make us happy. That can be like someone who eats to feel better, for comfort. The things themselves don't bring us long-lasting happiness; we may feel a sense of achievement and satisfaction for a while, but it's not long before we need something else to fill the void. It is the journey towards getting the thing we desire that is exciting. It is what we are becoming on our journey to our goal. It is the constant want for something new—our desires are always there; they are never ending. We enjoy the journey of creation, for being a co-creator is exciting. As mentioned aside from having goals we want to manifest and bring into our reality, we must also look at the internal for happiness, not just the external. If money was the answer to all our problems, then why is it that even for the ridiculously rich, it is not enough? By looking at the internal and connecting to our higher power, we are uniting with the wellbeing of the Universe to bring harmony and peace to ourselves. We mustn't constantly wait for other people to make us feel good, for they will constantly let us down. We are the main person to make ourselves feel good.

We learn to remember to be grateful for what we currently have while at the same time strive for what we want to come into our lives. Happiness and abundance are a state of mind, so as we realise the wealth of all that we do have, we feel happier, we are given the gift of happiness. Remember, we are given more of the same of what we are vibrating to. We are aligning with the very thing we want and so we allow more of the experience to come to us. Happiness is not about being happy with what you get: it's about being happy with what you've got. It is up to us to allow all our gifts to come to us, we must open to receive and not resist and push them away. Recognising our feelings in every area of our life is the key.

As mentioned when we recognise we have both positive and negative in ourselves, and that we feel a range of emotions, both light and dark, good and bad, positive and negative, that's when we can accept ourselves and our imperfections. We understand there is no perfection. We can't truly appreciate the heights of happiness without also experiencing pain or the depths of despair. When we've walked through the fires of hell, we can then again truly appreciate happiness and abundance (heaven). We appreciate love after we've been burnt and had our heart broken. We know day is always followed by night, winter always follows spring—it will always be this way. We will always feel a range of emotions as we go through the different seasons and stages in our lives. Life has both negative and positive times, highs and lows, ups and downs, ebb and flows and its cycles. So we must get rid of the illusion and fantasy that is portrayed in the happily-ever-after of fairytales and movies. Embrace our imperfections and dark side, but win it over with love and light and your good side.

4

Asking

Therefore I say to you whatever things you ask when you pray, believe that you receive them and you will have them. Mark 11:24

We must put our faith in our Higher Power and let go and let the Universe do its work. Don't be afraid to ask for help; don't try to be superman or superwoman and do everything on your own. Every successful business person or relationship knows that it is a team that makes things work or happen. Everybody who has achieved great things has done so with the assistance and help of others. Help is there if it is needed. All we have to do is ask. Whether it's support from your co-workers, partners, family, and friends; talking with a friend or family or a counsellor; reading the books; listening to the CDs or asking for help from the Universe, there is help out there. We all rely on each other. We are not separate; we are all connected and need each other for survival. Everything we use, have or own, everything we wear, everything we eat, or have in our houses, is made or grown by someone else. We all rely on one another to survive. Let people help you.

When we are down, we all need a helping hand to get back on our feet again. We don't want to be kicked in the gut when we are down. We need others that will help us get up. A successful partnership, whether it is a business, marriage or relationship, works because it is a team. They support each other, they know each others' strengths and weaknesses and utilise these to their advantage. And they know how to ask for help, and to give help when it's needed. It's the successful blending of the two personalities and characteristics that makes something work. It is the successful balancing of the others' imperfections that makes the partnership strong. Each of us striving for perfectionism only adds pressure and anxiety, so we must learn to ask for and accept help when we need it.

We all experience times when we feel we can never be good enough and we will never be able to measure up to unrealistic or fantasy ideals. In order to be happy we must release the expectation of perfection and accept that we are all imperfect. We are each a work in progress; we are constantly learning, changing, constantly evolving and expanding. We all have flaws and imperfections, and it is up to us to identify them, to make the most of our strengths, to work on our weaknesses, and to accept the things we can't change. This is another time to pick better-feeling thoughts about them.

We all have things we don't like about ourselves. Our job is to be grateful and happy with what we do have. Concentrate on what is good and work on and improve what we can improve and make better. When we learn to be happy with what we have and accept our and other people's imperfections, we release pressure and we release resistance. Perfection exists in magazines and in the movies. Don't just focus on all the bad and forget about all the good you have. Our aim is to work on our strengths and improve our weaknesses. Be grateful for what you do have, yet at the same time; strive for what you desire, and what you want. For when we do this, we feel good and open the floodgates and allow the good things to come to us.

Our daily task is to feel good as we release resistance and allow the good things we want to come to us. We can't change others or what is happening in the current moment. So we work on ourselves, and we choose better-feeling thoughts. That means we offer less resistance, so people and circumstances are able to change. People will begin to respond to us differently; our circumstances and the events around us start to change. Our thoughts make us feel better, and we have started the process. We know if we are resisting or aligning by checking in on how we are feeling. When we feel good we are in alignment, we are on track to bring in what we want. If we feel bad we are off track and out of alignment.

Surrender

Come to me, all you who are weary and burdened, and I will give you rest.
Matt 11:28

So do not fear, for I am with you; do not be dismayed, for I am your God. I will strengthen you and help you; I will uphold you with my righteous right hand.
Isa 41:10

Our negativity affects all the organs in our body. Learn to turn things over to the Universe because we are not meant to fight the battle alone, we are not meant to struggle towards our goals and to struggle in daily life. Leave the battle to God; leave it to the Universe. Tell the Universe your troubles or your plans, take action on your plans and then turn it over to our Higher Power to take care of. Move your ego aside, let go and allow the Universe to take over, organise or orchestrate all the details. Turn all your burdens over to God. When we are faced with obstacles and we feel overwhelmed by them, turn them over to the Universe, and stop resisting and fighting the battle ourselves. Worry, fear and anger are destructive; they are toxic to our minds, bodies and organs. Surrender your will and ask for God's will.

Let God carry our burdens on his shoulder instead of us carrying their weight on our own. They are heavy and a burden on our own. Ask God to help, and we will slowly feel the weight being lifted. When we are faced with adversity and huge challenges; and we don't know how or where to start to overcome things, ask God for help. For life sometimes throws us unexpected twists and turns, some may be so severe that we may find ourselves overwhelmed and out of faith. Both our hope and our faith have taken a beating and need to be restored. When you are trudging through life with a weary heart, learn to tell God your hopes, plans and desires. Let the God within give you the answers to heal you, your fears and worries. When life has packed you a punch and temporarily knocked you over, don't stay down for long; ask for help and turn it over to the Universe.

These affirmations are inspired by the work of Florence Scovel Shinn

Affirmations
I let God handle my burdens.
I am grateful for all the blessings that I have.
Things always work out for the best.
I am protected and safe and surrounded by love.
Whatever happens will be for my highest good.
The healer within now handles all my worries and fears.
I align with wellbeing and love.
Love, peace and wellbeing now surround me and heal the situation.
God walks with me through this situation.
I turn the situation over to God and the healer within.
God makes a way when there is no way.
I turn it over to the healer within.

Law of Karma

Karma is like a boomerang—what you give out comes back to you.
Rashida Rowe

Be aware that every action has a reaction. As we sow, so shall we reap in all our affairs. The way we treat others should be the way we want to be treated. If we judge others, we should expect people to judge us. If we talk kindly to others and about others and treat others with respect, we should expect the same in return. If we are rude, sarcastic or selfish, others will dislike, avoid or have resistance toward us. Maybe we won't always get what we want from some people as they are dealing with their own issues, or they may be self-centred, or have unrealistic expectations. But we will get what we want in some way or form from others in time. If we don't appreciate people and the help and support they give, expect resistance and the same in return. If we treat others badly then others will resist us, and treat us the same in return.

If we walk all over others then we will get resistance and conflict. If we have resistance, expect things and people to resist you. If others have done wrong by us, then I believe that Karma will catch up with them and they will eventually get their actions back in some way or form. Make it a conscious awareness that you behave according to your morals and values. Many times we don't get what we want from people because we are acting from our values and their values may be very different to ours. No one is perfect. However, we should all stick to treating others the way of the Bible.

Sometimes life is unfair and things beyond our control happen to us or to people around us. We were in the wrong place at the wrong time or it was just plain bad luck. We made a made an error in judgement, or a bad mistake and something ended up happening to us or someone else, and it's something we regret. Some things will remain a mystery and unexplained. Someone or some circumstance or tragedy may have caused us a great deal of pain, but it is up to us to slowly release our feelings of guilt, anger, hatred, resentment and revenge, and leave it to the Universe (Karma) so that we can heal and grow and move on. The more we hold onto our negative feelings, the more damage they do to us. We benefit when we let it go and move to a higher place. This is a process and requires facing the issue and pain and loss, work and persistence and of course time. If you find it difficult to do this, ask God to help you. We free ourselves when we forgive and cut ties.

Work on rebuilding your life, dreams or goals and hope again. We need to open ourselves and allow all the good we want to come in and let go of all the negative thoughts and feelings we hold inside of us: the hurt, anxieties, anger and fear, the worries and stresses. Heal those wounds and battle scars we have endured. Some scars may be so engrained they are like a tattoo etched into our heart so will take longer to heal. If we expect to see results in our life, we should be doing the work on ourselves, those necessary mental, emotional and physical disciplines. Plant the seed on fertile ground, water it daily, and watch it grow and have a life of its own. In time—if we continue to do the work and change the way we feel—we will see our rewards.

Goals

An idle mind is the devil's playground. Proverb
Keep your mind busy with the focus of a goal.

It is important for us to keep our goals and dreams alive, even when we are faced with huge challenges and obstacles and the future looks bleak. For without any goals, there is no hope; if there is no hope, there is no life and we will lose our drive, motivation or will. Hopes and goals keep us alive and keep us moving forward and growing. If we are not growing, we are wilting and stagnating. Goals focus us on the future; they focus us on where we want to go, not on what is happening in the now. Like a plant without any sun or water, a life without goals will eventually wilt and die. Goals are like the sun and water to our souls: they give us hope, they give us promise and dreams, and they give us a new lease on life. We feel excited to get out of bed every morning and face the day. Without hopes or goals there is nothing to strive for. But we need a direction. The soul always has desires. They are never-ending.

Keep a journal or notebook and write down your goals and record any affirmations, or anything that rings true to you or that you need to remember. Don't trust your memory. When you hear something good, make sure you write it down. Go over your journal or notebook regularly. Make a list of all your goals that you want to achieve in every area of your life. Have both short-term and long-term goals and revise your journal regularly. It is important to focus on what we want to attract into our lives, not on what we don't want.

The challenge is to learn to be happy with where we are right now, and to focus and strive for what is coming. When we move towards a new goal, a new desire or a new challenge, we are growing, we are expanding we are becoming more. Create goals for every area of your life, health, physical body, wealth, relationships and happiness. It is necessary to be aware that, while we strive for goals and are excited and look forward to the future, we must remember to live in the now and be present in the moment as much as we can. A person without a goal is like a person on a kayak without a paddle; they will drift to whatever destination or be tossed around by the turbulent waters of life. We need to grab those paddles and direct them to the destination we choose. At the same time, we need to be aware of the here and now, and of all that is good and living in the present moment.

Make a list of the desires you want to manifest. Be very specific with what you want. Write the date you want the goal achieved; clearly state the goal or desire or the amount of money you want. Then write down what you will give in return for what you want. You can use it in any area of your life: health, wealth, physical body, happiness, relationships, career, and any goals you desire. When we start to plan what we want in our lives, we will be the designers and co-creators of our own destiny.

By the date _____ I will _____. I will _____.

Read your list and visualise the outcomes daily.

Be conscious what words you are saying to yourself, and change them to better-feeling thoughts. We must choose thoughts that make us feel good about ourselves, so that we can feel better and attract more of the same into our lives. We must watch our words and thoughts, for they are powerful. At one point, I was going through a particularly challenging time, my separation, everything was breaking down in the house and I was finding it harder to be positive. The oven broke down, the thermostat on the hot water system broke, the coffee machine needed fixing, the TV was playing up, and two statues broke in the house. I was unconsciously sending out negative energy because of the negative state I was in. I realised what was happening and what I was doing and I started consciously sending positive thoughts out. Things started to settle down and eventually started falling into place. The quicker we get in tune with what is happening around us the quicker we can get back to changing our states.

When we feel we're not making progress towards our goal, we need to remember not to get stuck on, 'Why did this happen to me?' Ask, 'How can I be better? How can I be stronger? What can I learn from this situation?' Learn to ask better questions in order to find better solutions to your challenges and problems. Life is filled with a mixture of happiness, opportunity, challenges and obstacles for all of us. Life has its ups and downs for everyone; it is not reserved for just some people. There are good times and bad times. There are times of opportunity and difficulty for all of us. There are happy times and sad times for the rich, the middle class and the poor, the young and the old. The only people without problems are the people who are dead. Look at the situation and ask 'What can I take from this experience and learn?' or 'How can I apply it in my life and be of help to others?'

Things don't just happen, they happen for a reason. We can't control other people or some circumstances. However, we need to learn from our circumstances and certain situations and utilise them in our lives. Don't just learn from our own problems and challenges; learn from other people's success, problems or failures and use them in your life to move forward to a brighter future. Many people who have achieved great success in life have failed many times, or taken their obstacles and adversities and turned them into opportunity. Jim Rohn, Louise Hay, Og Mandino, Colonel Harland Sanders KFC, to name a few. Helen Keller became deaf and blind at 19 months of age and overcame all obstacles to become a successful author, and still inspires people to this day.

Law of gratitude

It's essential to focus on the wonderful things we have in our life. When we can't think of anything, we can put up some reminders of the good things we do have. Take out a picture of a time when you were happy, fit and healthy, or things were great. What about photos of the people you love and the things you have? We take many things for granted, especially our health. Imagine you had a terrible accident and you lost your ability to be independent in some way. What would you give for your eyesight, your kidneys, your lungs, your heart or the use of your brain—if you lost them? Our mind and body are magnificent: they do their job and we forget how blessed we are that everything just works perfectly. We mustn't take what we have for granted—we are blessed—we are far wealthier than we realise. There are always people worse off than we are at this moment. And there are many people who have managed to overcome their adversities and turn them into wonderful triumphs.

We have so many wonderful things to be grateful about, but for things to change for us, we must focus on what is good and what is working in our lives. Remember that our gratitude attracts more good into our lives; we feel happier and we begin to align to what we want. If we can sustain that good feeling it is only a matter of time what we want will come into our lives. If it seems to take longer than we expect, at least we are staying present and enjoying where we are at this moment. We can simply enjoy the ride while the current takes us toward our goal.

At times, the present can be too painful: that's the time to focus our thoughts on the future and what we want to achieve. As we work on building our faith and changing our thoughts and beliefs, we slowly move from our pain or grief to a feeling of hope, faith and then expectancy. We must keep our thoughts on what we want, not on what we don't want: the rules of attraction work for both the positive and the negative. When we focus on what we don't want, we bring more of the same (negative experience) into our world. When we focus on what we do want, we are not focusing on the now (of what you don't have), but on what we want to manifest and bring into our lives.

There will always be times when we want something else, or there's a new goal to achieve. We must not forget that while we use positive affirmations and visualisations to bring what we want into our life remember to also to focus on the now, express our gratitude for it, and not miss this present moment. Focusing on the now enables us to focus and appreciate all the wonder and the good things and wellbeing of the Universe. That will help connect us to our source and help bring our desires into our life, while enjoying the current experiences, and not let life just pass us by. Living in a state of awareness helps us do this. The reminders we put up around our house help keep us on track.

Use anchors that will remind us to be grateful every day

- A song, a saying, a picture, a book.
- An affirmation, a visualisation.
- A clipping of something that reminds you of something your grateful about.
- A picture of something you want to achieve.
- A memento of a special experience.
- A photo, a quote or a poem.

When we learn to move to a state of gratitude, to change our negative thoughts to positive thoughts, to develop faith and have hope in life and the Universe, we unlock the door to the gifts that life has for us and we and are wide open to receive them.

Affirmations
I give thanks to the Lord for all my blessings.
Thank you, God. I see you working in my life.
I open the door to my wellbeing and I am grateful for all that I have.
I am grateful for all the abundance in my life.
I open the floodgates to my abundance now.

Law of giving

We are here to help, contribute, give and serve others. This can be done in a variety of ways, as a parent, a friend, a business, or giving our time in helping others or monetary donations. It may be as a teacher, it may be as guidance, or as emotional support. It may be you are part of a team at work or on the sports field. You may be an artist, a doctor or a gardener. We all can contribute and give to others. However, we must also remember to give to ourselves, for what good are we to others if we are constantly stressed, tired and irritable? The last thing we want to do is help others when we ourselves feel that way. By looking after ourselves and by taking the time to do the things we enjoy, to de-stress and balance ourselves, we then in turn can help others better. When we are constantly giving to others, we run out of fuel. So remember to refuel ourselves first, so we can be a better person for everyone else. When we remember that we are our first priority and we look after ourselves, we are in a better position to give the best of ourselves; our energy, moods and concentration will be higher and better. Then we can think what we could do to help or benefit others. While we may not be able to give monetary donations, we can give our time; we can give our attention and love. We can give a friendly smile, a kind word, an encouraging gesture. These small acts of kindness make a big difference in someone else's life. Helping others whether it's one person, a family or a community makes us feel good about ourselves and we make a difference.

I remember once when I had to get a whole lot of presents packed and sent to Sydney for Christmas, the post office was packed with a long line of stressed customers. A kind man heavily covered in tattoos offered to hold my huge box the whole time I waited in line; he could see it was heavy and it would have been hard for me. Well, his small, thoughtful, respectful act of kindness made my day. A small act of kindness goes a long way. We all can help each other, put a smile on the other person's face, and make people feel special. When we are stressed and anxious, we come from a place of fear and worry. When we are calm and relaxed we come from a place of love. Remember the saying, 'we change the world with one small act of kindness.' One act of kindness goes a long way and is paid forward. Act according to your morals and values, don't just react to others. If others have treated you badly getting revenge or hurting them is not the answer. If we can all remember to act according to the teachings of the Bible then we can change the world. Remember you make a difference, one act of kindness will make someone happy and feel special and they will pay it forward. And you will feel good in helping someone and even better the good will come back around to you. You will get the good come back to you by someone else in some way or form.

5

Aligning And Receiving

Accept what is and go with the flow of life.
Keep your mind busy with the expectation of the best.

Our emotions are our guidelines. When we are feeling not so good—we need to look at what we are saying to ourselves and change it to good-feeling thoughts. When we feel good, we are telling ourselves good thoughts and have good beliefs and feelings; we are aligning. Just as when we are feeling bad, we are resisting and not letting all the good we want to come into our lives; we are pushing it away. In feeling good we are pulling the good towards us and letting it in.

Imagine knocking on a door waiting for someone to open it for you—but it's locked and no one is there to open it. You try and try to open the door, you push, you shove, but it's jammed tight. That's exactly what happens when we resist situations. We fight, we push, we are stuck, and we don't move. But when we align it's as if we don't need anyone to open the door for us. WE have the key. We put the key in and the door opens. Working out how to open the door takes practice; it requires repetition, discipline and persistence to reach the feeling (vibration) of what we want and become one with it (aligning).

When we stop resisting things, people, events and circumstances and start aligning to our wellbeing, our energy will change. Resisting pushes things away from us: aligning brings things to us. When we resist a situation we magnify it, making it bigger. When we cease to be bothered by it, and concentrate on feeling good, we are aligning, and feeling better – and things begin to change. Circumstances and people around us change and more good comes into our lives.

The more we fight life, the more life becomes difficult. You may not even realise you are resisting, as it may be done on a subconscious level. When we fight people or circumstances, when we want to punish people or get revenge for hurting us, we're making the situation worse. It's only in accepting things, people or what is and letting go and forgiving that we are able to heal and move forward.

That's why it's so important to be aware of how we feel about a situation, person or circumstance. Go with the flow, don't try to swim against the current, align with it, join with it and let the current take us where we want to go. How much harder is it when you are riding your bike against the wind, especially on a windy day? It is far more difficult, than when the wind is behind you pushing you—the wind helps you; the ride is far easier. That is what happens when we fight: it is as if we ride against the wind; we push against a brick wall; things get harder. Nothing good can get in; there is a blockage. Learn to go with the flow of life, by aligning and not resisting.

We have done the asking. Now we must allow all the good we want to come into our lives. We must get into a better-feeling place to attract what we want: good health, a desire for a better body, more peace, harmony, happiness and wellbeing, better relationships. Whatever it is that we want to bring into our lives, we must first look at how we are feeling about that particular area. Don't push, fight, struggle or resist. Aligning with the feeling allows us to receive it.

Love and Deserving

Love is the most powerful force in the Universe. Love is what binds us all together. Love and respect hold marriages, partnerships or friendships together. Love is everything that is good. Love has the power to heal, grow and create miracles. When we feel love for ourselves we can more easily love others. If we find it hard to love our self, we must practise affirming that we love ourselves and that we deserve to receive what we want. There is plenty of happiness, health, wealth and success to go around. When we believe in abundance, we won't feel bad if we have or others have success, money or good relationships, or reach our goals when others don't. When we feel lack, we may feel guilty or not worthy: that causes us to cut ourselves off from our supply. We are all worthy and deserving.

Practise saying you love yourself and you deserve to have what you want; say it over and over until it becomes a belief. Affirm it in your mind, say it out loud or chant it. Do whatever it takes to change those thoughts that are holding you back. If we feel guilt, regret, or bad about ourselves, it's time to heal those old thoughts, scars, wounds and beliefs, and replace them with new ones. We must let go of those toxic feelings of anger, resentment or hatred; they are holding us back and we won't be able to move forward and cut ties completely until we forgive and release them out to the Universe.

All healing begins first in the mind and on the internal. Healing begins when we love ourselves and want to make changes and want to be better. Loving ourselves means we don't have to put up with behaviour we don't want or that constantly makes us feel bad. Loving ourselves means disassociating from negative people, circumstances or situations. Loving ourselves means standing up for ourselves when we need to; our health, wellbeing and sanity demand it. We must put our health first. Loving ourselves means realising when negative or toxic patterns or relationships play havoc with our peace of mind, health and wellbeing. Maybe we won't ever forget but we let go and forgive and release the toxic feelings.

We must believe in our own power within and trust that the Universe will provide. Many times we may want things, but our lack of self-love or worthiness is actually stopping things from entering our lives. Many times we are too scared of the unknown to take the first step to change things. For the sake of our peace, health and wellbeing, we must put ourselves first and look after ourselves. Love breaks down when there is no respect, there is a lack of empathy, is shown no appreciation, is taken for granted, mistreated or abused. Or relationships can break down when someone stops making an effort, is one-sided or treats the other person badly.

We all repeat our patterns of conditioning from early childhood to some extent, as this is how we learn and respond. Many times we do it subconsciously and it is not until we are older that we see and hear ourselves repeat what our parents used to do and say. Our values are taught to us from a young age by our parents or caretakers, by what we saw and what we learnt as acceptable behaviour. People who have been damaged or exposed to abuse can ruin or wreck us—if they repeat their family patterns of conditioning. Some may inflict their injuries on you as they've been wounded and scarred and learnt a certain way of coping. Unless they have dealt with their issues; and have healed them. However we all make choices as to how we act or how we treat people. Some times in order to protect ourselves, we may have to walk away from these relationships. Doing so is no easy task and is a hard decision to make when we love the people or enjoy our friendships—yet realise their patterns are causing us harm. Otherwise we may end up sacrificing our health, wellbeing and peace of mind. This may be a decision you need to consider as toxic relationships cause toxic outcomes. God wants us to be happy, and seek the 'promised land' as mentioned in the Bible, if we are in bondage (enslavement). God wants us to have respect for ourselves, have healthy boundaries and love and treasure our minds and bodies. Just as an addict loves the drug but comes to realise that it's no good and will eventually destroy them—we must understand how important it is ceasing toxic patterns and look at having healthy and positive patterns and habits.

Make sure you have your support group around you if you do decide to make changes. As you will need to have people around you who will give you emotional support, while you make changes and set boundaries. Sometimes distance may force the other person to accept your changes, and because of their pain, they will have to change as well. Sometimes when we change and won't put up with behaviour that makes us feel bad and set boundaries, we risk the real chance of losing friendships, relationships or our jobs—as many people may not be able to accept our changes. Decide if this is something that you are willing to risk and work on changing yourself. You will get external as well as internal resistance. As the internal patterns of our family upbringing (conditioning)—feelings of guilt, or fear will raise its ugly head and try to keep things the same (enslavement). So be prepared for a struggle with others as well as yourself and your old conditioned thoughts and habits. Many times if we are trying to stop negative or destructive patterns we may need to disassociate from these situations or people in order to gain the strength to stop the negative habit or pattern. Sometimes this may be for a while until we are strong enough and have conditioned our new habits, or sometimes we may have to completely cut ties.

Things we must do when we make changes:

- Talk to friends and family for support.
- Join or have an emotional support network that can help you with your issue. As you will align with like-minded people they will help support you as you gain strength as you are changing.
- Enlist the help of a professional that deals with your particular issue.
- Read books, study all you can about what you want to improve.
- Talk to a counsellor to help you with strategies, healing and forgiveness.
- Read or put up positive affirmations while you are changing, to keep you hopeful.
- Do things that make you happy.
- Take one day at a time.
- Look after yourself by eating well and resting.
- Exercise to release good feeling endorphins and release stress.
- Meditate or sit in quietude for 15 minutes daily.
- Ask for God's help.
- Keep on persisting as you will fall back into your old ways some times.
- Keep practising your new patterns until they become a habit.
- Attend church for positive messages and emotional support.
- If you don't attend church work on your faith and connection with Divine Power.
- DO NOT give up even if you fall back in your old patterns.

Loving ourselves means setting up boundaries as to how we wish to be treated and what we want to attract and have in our life. Loving ourselves means taking time out for us and doing things that make us feel good: meditation, walking in nature, exercise, a hobby, whatever is right for each of us. Loving ourselves means respecting our body and watching what foods we put into our body so we feel good and energetic. We are all worthy to have the things that makes us happy in our life; it's up to us to decide what these are and believe we deserve them. And take that leap of faith.

If you end up losing faith in life, love or people, we must put our faith in God and believe in life's possibilities again. When things have been broken, lost, damaged or your world has been shattered and turned upside down, it takes time to heal, rebuild and re-create the new. Don't lose hope. Survivors keep on getting up no matter how many times they've been thrown down. Believe in love, for love creates the new. Hope, faith and love must endure in our soul—when it fades or dies it must be re-ignited by us. By us making a conscious choice, to believe in life again and its endless opportunities.

Mind/Ego – Personality

Only when your mind and body are in the same place you are present, you are in the moment of now.

We are in the moment when our mind and body align in the same place. So make it a practice to be in the moment as often as you can— use all your senses, sight, touch, smell and hearing and taste; use your (mind) thoughts to connect and experience the moment. Our mind (ego) has a purpose: to work out solutions to problems, to plan and to analyse things. We are meant to use it at will, not let it run rampant; we are to restrict its hold on us; we need to limit its attacks, control and harassment. We must have constant vigilance on our thoughts.

Are you fearful, stressed or anxious, or are you easygoing, calm or confident? Maybe you are spontaneous, broad-minded or rigid? Or are you a glass half full or a glass half empty personality? Are you giving or are you self-centred? We can tend towards one or more most of the time, and we can probably have some or a few of those characteristics

77

in our personalities at different times in our lives—depending on what we are going through at the different stages in our lives. When we are stressed or fearful or angry, we are more likely to react. When we are peaceful and balanced, we are more likely to be easygoing, calm and not bothered. When we get hurt and feel insecure, we may be more likely to react or get upset. However it is important to recognise which category we mostly fall into, whether it's the positive personalities or the negative more of the time. The way we feel is our experience and our perceptions about the things that are happening in our world. The way we feel is our reality.

Being self-confident and having a healthy ego, self-respect and a healthy sense of ourselves are important to the way we treat ourselves and let others treat us. It is when we get lost in the ego that we get lost in the separateness of the personality and forget the wonder, miracle and oneness of life and the Universe. When we are stuck in our personality and always have to prove we are right, try to control, or never hear or listen to anyone else—that is when we are lost in the personality and feel separate and isolated.

Some people can be extremely egotistical or narcissistic. It is hard to recognise these people as they wear a mask of niceness and are people pleasers initially on the outside. No one really knows what they are like behind closed doors. They may seem easy going but in reality are demanding, have unrealistically high expectations and are overly critical. Nothing is ever good enough. They tend to look at things from a different perspective. They look at things that haven't been done and miss everything that's been done. Some people may be controlling using threats to get their way. Others may punish you when their needs are not met, pout, sulk or withdraw emotionally. Look at and be aware of what you are allowing and how you are being treated or the way you are treating others.

Many people stuck in the ego/mind personality need to constantly think they are right, no matter what. It is draining, overpowering and hard work to constantly appease and try to please them. They may tend to blame others as they are always right, and can never do anything wrong. Some have no understanding or empathy for anything other than what is happening in their own life. Others are so self-centred and everything is about them. They always have to win and their negative patterns can have a tight grip on them—and on us if we're not vigilant. They are so entrenched in this pattern they don't know any other way and, worse still, they keep on falling back into these negative patterns and can suck us into a downward spiral, if we are not careful.

The mind personality lives in the past or future, not in the present. So many people stuck in the mind/personality find it hard to let go, forgive and move forward. Avoiding looking at our shortcomings, faults and mistakes doesn't allow us to work on our issues and fix them in order to become better, to learn from them and not keep on repeating them. Also when we are stuck in the mind, we can be so focused on finding solutions or fixing things that are bothering us and we are so absorbed on that, we can't focus on anything else. So we miss the now. We can be so stuck on past hurts and resentments that we keep on replaying them over and over like a broken record. Don't let yourself be stuck on the past, we need to move that needle forward ourselves when it gets jammed on the record player, and won't move from that place. Learn to be aware if you feel you are getting sucked into the personality, someone else's personality or any negative energy. **Pause**, take deep breaths and remember to change your focus. Don't react. When we are angry, when we are emotionally charged we say things we don't mean, or do things irrationally.

Ways to avoid people stealing your energy or reacting:

You will need an anchor or an ice-breaker. So pick something that will work for you.

- Practise the 'pause'. Feeling our body tensing is the signal to stop, and to pause. Breathe. Take 5 to 10 long deep breaths and use an anchor to change our negative thoughts to positive thoughts—one step at a time.
- *I know he doesn't mean it when he acts like that.*
- *She does try to get along sometimes, she is only 16, and I was like that at her age.*
- *I remember it was difficult at her age, trying to find ourselves.*
- If things are getting heated tell them that you will talk or discuss things later,
- Walk away until you have calmed down, no matter how long it takes—20 minutes, 1 hour or a couple of hours.
- Put on some music, or do some exercise.
- I find doing some physical work helpful to release the negative energy.
- Do something else to distract you if you can. What do we do to a child when they are crying? We try and change their focus or distract them with something else.
- Do whatever we can to try to get our focus on something else.
- The quicker we can change our focus and our negative thoughts to better-feeling thoughts, the quicker we will get back to feeling good again.
- When we feel we are ready, it's time to try to talk to the other person.
- Be prepared that just because you are ready to talk to them rationally and calmly they may not be and it may take them a lot longer.

Example of ego thoughts that pull you away—and how to recover

Imagine you are at the most beautiful place, say your favourite beach. It's a beautiful day, but all you can think about are the problems you have had at work, the argument you just had, or the deadlines you have to meet. Your body is there physically but your mind is elsewhere; it's simply not there. When our mind and body are connected and we can focus our awareness on where we are, then we are truly in the moment to appreciate things; to feel, touch or smell and notice things.

- Learn to stop, pause and use as many of your senses as you can to bring you in alignment with the moment.
- Take in the sights, smells, sounds, beauty and connect to people and nature; connect yourself to the experience.
- Appreciate what you do have and focus your thoughts on the good things in your life. Focus on things that are working, and be grateful.
- Resist the mind's attempts to distract you with thoughts of things to do, thoughts of past, present and future.

It's a given that it's much harder to do this when things are particularly challenging. However, we must remain in a state of awareness and mindfulness in order for things to change.

Once we have become aware of our negative-feeling thoughts and positive-feeling thoughts, and have written out new ones to replace the old thoughts and beliefs, we need to change our negative patterns of resisting to positive patterns of aligning.

The way we act and react depends on our personality, our values and what we are going through at that particular time, whether we are feeling peaceful, happy and in alignment, or stressed, exhausted, fearful or depressed and out of alignment. We can tend to be more of one personality most of the time, however, what we are going through does affect the way we react to things. The quicker we become aware of what we are thinking and saying to ourselves and what we are feeling, the quicker we can move from a bad-feeling place to a good-feeling place. Then we can slowly start feeling good again and can enjoy our experiences more, and allow the good things we want to come into our lives.

We give our energy and our power away by the way we react to people or to circumstances. We make ourselves feel bad or feel sick when we get upset. So it's important that we must have a constant security guard at the door of our mind. We must make it a conscious effort to protect ourselves, our energy and our wellbeing, to avoid negativity or conflict, and to disassociate from people who constantly bring us down, or make us feel bad. With all the stress, pressure and demands on us, we need to surround ourselves with happy, positive, like-minded and well-intentioned people. Some people are hell bent on always being right, being difficult and want everything their way. When we choose peace and harmony, when we choose aligning rather than resisting, and cease any toxic patterns, we start putting us first and taking responsibility for ourselves and our wellbeing.

Our thoughts are things that send out frequencies. The more we think about something, the more energy we send it. It works for both positive and negative. When we send good thoughts out, we send out good, positive energy (aligning); we attract more of the good we want to come. When we send out bad thoughts, we send out negative energy (resisting) and attract more of that bad experience into our life and keep that experience in our life. The more we focus on something that upsets us or makes us feel bad, the more it stays the same and magnifies. Keeping a check on our feelings indicates what track we are on. We all fall into negative patterns subconsciously, without realising what we are actually doing and saying. Remember keep a constant vigilant check on how we are feeling.

Conditioning negative patterns to positive patterns

We are what we repeatedly do. Excellence, therefore, is not an act, but a habit. Aristotle

When we realise the most important thing we can do for ourselves is to choose to feel good daily, we take responsibility for our wellbeing. We develop better beliefs about ourselves and our lives. When we choose peace and harmony, we align with the Universe, and we will have less stress and more of all the things we want. We enjoy things more, and more things can flow through us. When we retreat from arguments, conflict or ego/personality and let things go, we feel better.

As mentioned sometimes no matter what we do or how hard we try, we find some people who are unconsciously stuck in their ego and negative patterns. We may have to avoid or remove ourselves from unpleasant situations, instead choosing peace and harmony. Many of the struggles we have are internal beliefs that have been conditioned by our upbringing, our own personal make-up and what we were taught and exposed to at an early age.

Be aware that when we start to heal ourselves, our mind will try to keep its strong hold on us to keep things the same. Keep in mind also that when we try and change people will resist and fight you in order to keep things the same. As mentioned, people don't like change and they may not accept you and your changes. That is a real risk we must take, and we must decide if it is worth the risk of losing the friends, relationships or the jobs we have. Only you can answer that question. But for us to be better and happier, not repeat the same patterns, heal, move forward and expand WE must change. We need practice, repetition and persistence daily to break the old patterns to change to our new thoughts, beliefs and patterns.

Some people may react to you with rage, some will try to make you feel guilty, fearful, or may punish you. Some people may eventually accept the new you, some may not. Others may object and make you feel guilty for looking after yourself, having an opinion, saying no or for standing up for yourself or what you believe. Do not fall back into the old ways and the old thinking.

Techniques on helping you as you are changing:

- Remember don't ask why, ask, 'How can I be better'?
- What can I do to change or what can I do differently?
- Try another approach to get the results you want.
- Know exactly what it is you want to bring in your life that you don't have now.
- Work on yourself.
- Read books, study what you need to learn or attain.
- What or who must I avoid?
- Persistence—keep on trying till you get stronger and develop the habit.
- Have your emotional support network in place and call or see them when needed, be it friends or family, a counsellor or someone who deals specifically with your issue.
- Look after yourself as we have mentioned previously.
- Do things that make you feel happier.
- Ask God for help, pray, ask God to give you the strength you need.
- Attend church or the spiritual group you believe in, or if you don't attend church, develop and strengthen your connection to Divine Power.
- Exercise to release stress and feel better.
- Meditate, or practice deep breathing.
- Take time out in a quiet corner where you can align and be in the now.

Remember you may keep on falling into the same negative patterns even when you are trying to change and aware what you need to change, just stick to what you are doing and eventually with practice, repetition and discipline the new pattern will become a habit.

Again, it's important to remember you will need to be prepared to have an internal battle as well as external battle. Some people may react with anger or try to regain control, some may cut you off, as they are used to getting everything their way. Or some people may eventually accept your changes. You may have to distance yourself from negative situations or people till you get stronger. You may have to walk away from friends, partners, or negative situations if they cannot accept your changes. Use your support network while you are working on changing as they will help provide the strength and assistance you need while you change.

When I was living in Sydney I had panic attacks after my second daughter was born. The counsellor called it perinatal stress all the stress of moving houses twice while I was pregnant, working full time on my job and part time on my business and the birth of my daughter caused me to start having anxiety attacks after she was born. With study, and understanding as to why I was experiencing this negative thought pattern, practice, repetition and awareness to break these anxiety attacks, I broke the negative habit and haven't had panic attacks for over 14 years.

The more we can remain conscious of our thoughts when we are feeling bad, the more in control we will be to diffuse the negative energy—not take it on, or simply not give it our energy. It's when we are unaware of our thoughts and feelings that we are more likely to react, or fall into negative habits. So practise awareness. Make the here-and-now the most important moment, not the past and future. Our mind loves to dwell in the past and in the future: it always tries to distract us from this moment.

When we are in the moment, we are connected to our source and all that is good. When we constantly remain in the mind, we are connected to timelines, demands, things to do, pressure, pain, suffering and challenges. Use your mind at will—for when you need to use it at work, or to plan or work out solutions. But don't let it use you. Remain aware, in the present as much as you can. If you forget and slip up, get back to feeling good as quickly as possible. When we're in the present we tend to be grateful, appreciative and loving; we notice the beauty, wonder and magic of life. We get insights, we are open to miracles, we are trusting and have hope and faith. Whatever the moment, experience it. Stop fighting it; let it touch you. There is a time to laugh, to cry or be happy, to feel sorrow and grief, and to face our challenges and adversities.

When you feel trapped in a tunnel of darkness and you see a glimmer of light—no matter how small—follow its path of promise (hope), and it will slowly get brighter and brighter. If you hold onto this, in time you will have the faith, courage and the strength to be able to climb out to the top of the mountain, and you will feel the warm glow of the sun and be surrounded by light once again. Open yourself to receive this feeling and allow the experience to penetrate your soul, and hold onto that energy.

We must look at and observe our patterns of resistance, and change them to patterns of aligning. At times, we all fall into negative patterns without even realising we're doing it. When we want things to change, we need to look at what we are actually saying to ourselves and to others, what we are feeling, doing and what patterns we are falling into. Are we allowing people or the things we want, to come closer to us, or are we resisting and pushing them away? We must also look at and observe our patterns and see if we are treating others the way we want to be treated and look at how we are allowing others to treat us.

Positive patterns. Aligning (Higher Self). Glass half-full

Love	Gratitude
Harmony	Abundance
Peace	Centred, Balanced
Joy	Easygoing
Happiness	Decisive
Excitement	Giving
Strength, Power	Relaxation
Forgiving	Secure
Hope	Responsibility
Empathetic	Faith
Honesty	Boundaries
Trust	Contentment
Respect	Caring
Compliment, Praise	Appreciating, Valuing
Broad minded	Confidence

Negative patterns. Resisting (Mind/Ego/Personality). Glass half-empty

Arguments, Conflict	Insecurity
Blame	Lack of trust
Judgement	Criticism
Stubbornness	Indecision
Disrespect	Boredom
Loneliness	Anxiety
Anger	Controlling
Worry	Jealousy
Fear	Depression
Weakness, Powerlessness	No hope or faith

Resentment	Ungrateful
Rigid, narrow minded	Self-centred
Deceiving	Manipulative
Lack of empathy	No boundaries
Unforgiving	Abusive
Hatred	Guilt
Revenge, punish	Withdrawal, Isolation
Sabotage	

We need to exercise our minds by being aware of what we are feeling, what we are thinking, what we are doing and how we are acting or reacting. If our feelings and thoughts are off track, we need to use the techniques we've learnt to change the negative thought patterns to positive thought patterns and get back on track. We must recognise not only our negative patterns, but others' negative patterns and change them to positive patterns. Otherwise, things will stay the same or get worse. There will be challenging times, when it is harder for you to control your thoughts. However, if you are aware that nothing is more important for you, than your wellbeing, then you need to constantly check in on how you are feeling. When we are aware that our emotions guide us, we need to monitor our thoughts, and change them to better-feeling thoughts and patterns, using the techniques we've learnt earlier. This is when you need to be vigilant in your attempts to get back on track with good-feeling thoughts and patterns. The more we practise, the more aware we become. Doing tai chi, yoga, meditation and any exercise are excellent activities to help balance the mind, body and spirit.

If you are feeling fearful about a certain situation

Be aware of how you react to things so you can change this pattern. In being aware, we can identify our negative thought patterns, start to break their hold, and change them to better ways. We need to work on ourselves if we want to see changes. Being aware makes us more in control, and allows us to practise the techniques to change our negative patterns. Challenge our thoughts with new thoughts; replace our negative ways with better ways. When we're unaware, we stay stuck in our patterns and trapped in our mind/personality.

When we move into awareness, when we are conscious of our strengths, our weaknesses, the way we feel, the way we are, and the way we act or react. WE can change things. We learn from our successes and our mistakes by reflection, doing the work and by mindfulness, by being the observer from a distance.

We may not feel like changing our negative-feeling thoughts to good-feeling thoughts, because it is a discipline. And being mindful and working on ourselves is much harder to do when we are feeling bad, depressed, or miserable. But if we do this enough and push through, our energy state will eventually start to change, and we will start to feel better. In feeling better, we are aligning more good to come us; and our new thought will eventually turn into a belief. Once we have reached the vibration of that belief, what we want will eventually manifest in our lives.

If you feel fearful, that something bad might happen (negative-feeling thought)
Replace it with good-feeling thoughts

I am safe and protected.
I am now free from all fear and worry, and the Universe protects me I am safe.
God protects us all.

If you haven't already, write out your new thoughts about the things you want to change and bring into your life.

Affirmations

All my relationships are harmonious.

I now have perfect health.

Everything will work out for the best.

I am strong and healthy and full of energy.

My body knows how to heal itself back to its perfect state.

I give thanks for my abundance.

I release all guilt and worry.

God walks with me through this, I am safe.

All I want comes to me now.

I am now open to all the good I want.

I open up to receive my good now.

6

Getting Started

Taking action

Repetition is the mother of skill. Jim Rohn

It's all very well and good to have positive thoughts and positive affirmations. Without action, nothing will happen. We need to do the work: read the books, listen to the CDs, exercise, watch what foods we put into our bodies, and take time out to rest. We make the time to meditate, re-energise our mind and connect to our higher self. And WE need to change our patterns. We discipline ourselves and motivate ourselves to take the actions that will bring us the things we want in our lives. We must use our mental muscles daily and take the necessary steps in order to make our dreams come true.

Changing our thoughts, getting into the feeling state and visualising what it is we want is only one half of the equation. We can't just sit down all day and expect it is going to just show up: we put a plan in place and take the steps to make it happen. We are the one who exercises; it won't work if someone else does it for us. We watch what foods we put into our bodies; we do the meditations; and we are the one who plants the seed of desire and make sure we water it daily. First we plant the seed and we ensure we water it daily, and then it takes root and starts to sprout. It grows and becomes stronger; we maintain it with our daily awareness and care. Soon it's the beautiful plant it was meant to become. So we create our desire, first in the form of thought, then we take the actions in the physical world. Most people know what to do, but not everyone does what they should do. It takes discipline to do it consistently: small steps on a daily basis will bring good health and wellbeing and all that we want to manifest in our life.

Most people want money, but money without health is useless. Our health is the priority that we need to focus on. Our body is a magnificent machine. It is only when we lose our health that we realise what we actually do have and take for granted every day. It's one of those things that, sometimes we don't realise the treasure we have until it is taken away from us. So we must remember to be grateful for our health, and always make it our first priority. We have everything we need inside of us.

When I was in my early stages of treatment and didn't know how things would turn out, a lady I knew came to visit me and brought me a gift and with it a lottery scratchy which gave me the chance to win fifty thousand dollars. If I had had the choice, which would I choose between—the money or my health? Well in that precise moment, I realised what was more important, I wanted my health back, I wanted to live. There is more to life than work and just accumulating things, life is also all about enjoying our experiences. Having money to enjoy the lifestyle you desire is one thing, but there are many types of wealth.

We may see the good we have and do the best we can, but we don't actually see the gold and the treasure that lies buried deep within each and every one of us. It needs to be awakened and put to use. We don't need to look elsewhere or outside to find it, we must find it in inside of us and unlock its power. We can have all the money in the world and be unhappy, feel lonely, depressed, miserable or have ill health. Real wealth and happiness is about recognising we have everything that we need and being grateful for what we have, whilst we strive for the things we want to bring into our life.

So develop a plan and take the actions required to get you to your desired goal. We always want new things and new experiences; it is natural for us to have new desires. Once we reach a new goal or dream that we wanted, it is not too long before we have the longing for a new desire. If we only wait to be happy when we achieve things, we will never be happy for long. Be happy in the now, it is the journey of where we are heading, what we are becoming, and how we are growing that is the real excitement. Focus your thoughts on everything you do have that is good in your life—your loved ones, careers or jobs, your health, where you live, the wonderful country you live in and all of the opportunities that are available to us. Be grateful for what you do have in your life and experience the excitement and joy of the journey towards the goal.

Diet

Let food be thy medicine and medicine be thy food. Socrates

Many books about food focus solely on what types of foods we should (or shouldn't) eat, what portions we must have and what vitamins and minerals we should take. We can find countless recipes to cook so that we can maintain a good state of health and wellbeing. We all know what we must eat, but we don't always do what we should do. Our lifestyles are fast paced and busy, so it's easy to take shortcuts.

However to have and maintain optimum health and wellbeing, we must provide our bodies with a good balance of fruit and vegetables, protein, carbohydrates, fibre and calcium, vitamins and minerals, and essential fats. They are essential to maintain our body weight and to keep our cells and organs functioning properly, as well as giving us the mental and physical stamina to do all the things we want to do. Food is the fuel we need to give us the energy and stamina to carry out our tasks throughout the day, in order for us to keep up with the demands of life.

Are we putting E10, unleaded or premium unleaded fuel into your body? I believe we should aim for premium by eating as much natural and organic food, free-range eggs and meats, and hormone-free meats as your budget allows. Many people are going back to nature and growing at least some of their own produce or herbs. We can top up our food intake with essential oils, vitamins and mineral supplements from the many fabulous naturopaths or health food stores, or health food sections in supermarkets or pharmacies.

I've said it before: it is imperative for us to look after ourselves. Foods that are high in fat cause our body to feel sluggish because it is using all the energy to digest our food. Keep foods high in sugar to a minimum as these tend to give us quick boost and then a drop in energy levels. Look for low-GI foods as these give a more sustained energy release. Eating fresh raw foods gives our body the life force energy it needs to feed our cells, so they function correctly and perform better. The demands of our lives makes it is easy to get caught up with the thought that there's not enough time to prepare and cook meals all the time. However, it is essential for our minds and bodies, as well as our emotional levels that we respect and look after ourselves, including the way we eat. We are responsible for what we put in—as we decide what we put into our bodies. If we want to feel good, we need to eat the foods that will give us the energy, the ability to focus and the stamina to get what we want done.

Just as toxic thoughts are bad for us, junk foods, highly processed foods full of preservatives, foods high in sugar and fat are acidic to our body. We need to provide both our mind and body with mostly alkaline foods, and these are found in all the good foods that nature provides for us. Remember alkaline vs. acidic—if it's alkaline it's good for you, have as much as you can, most people say 80% of your diet, aim for a minimum of 70%. If it's acidic, keep your intake of these foods to a minimum.

Moderation is the key, nothing to excess. What foods we put into our body determines how we will feel during the day. If we eat junk food most or all of the time, we cannot expect to feel energetic, but tired and lethargic as our body tries its best to digest and break down the food. Side effects of junk food, highly processed foods, or foods high in fat or sugar include weight gain, diabetes or clogging organs and arteries. Be aware and be guided by how you feel: if you feel bad eating certain foods, cut them out of your diet and increase foods that make you feel good and more energetic and more vital.

Raw fruits and vegetables contain the life force energy and provide our body with the vitamins and nutrients needed in order for it to function effectively. If you steam or boil vegetables, don't overcook them as this tends to destroy their essential vitamins (they need only a few seconds). Stir-frying is an excellent option. Drink freshly squeezed raw juices daily or as often as possible. Drink purified, filtered or bottled water as much as you can or most of the time, 6 to 8 glasses a day. Swap your fizzy drinks for water, which is the most vital nutrient to give oxygen to our cells and organs. Try to eliminate or keep to a minimum any toxins, preservatives, pesticides and sugar. Keep processed fast foods to a minimum and substitute honey for sugar when you can. If you have a filter in your house rinse vegetables and fruit in this water as there are many nasty toxins in our water. Try to cut down or keep salt to a minimum as this retains water. Include probiotics, such as acidophilus and bifidus, in your diet to promote healthy gut bacteria.

Cut down or cut out caffeine; substitute for tea or herbal teas as these contain antioxidants. Have a multivitamin as a supplement if you want or need to. In our technology age we are surrounded by radiation from computers, TVs, mobile phones, microwaves, radios, alarm clocks and wireless infrared signals. Be aware and minimise your exposure to these radiations, as they do affect our personal energy fields. Use ear pieces or hands free if you use mobiles frequently for long periods; use computer screen filters if you use computers for long periods and sit at a distance from TV screens.

What price are you willing to pay in return for what it is you desire? If it's good health, we must watch what foods we put into our bodies. If it's so you can feel better, what are you doing about it? If you want to keep your weight to a healthy level for your body type, are you exercising and eating foods that are good for you? Are you drinking soft drinks, lots of coffees, or do you drink mostly water or herbal teas? Junk food must be kept to an absolute minimum, as a reward or as a treat. Our bodies and minds need good fuel to function and perform at their best in order to maintain a healthy body, health and wellbeing.

Our bodies and minds are marvelous: let's treat them with the respect they deserve. We need to pay attention to ourselves, our needs, our diet and our exercise. What kind of foods do you put into your body? Are you always tired, or are you energetic? Are you too busy and put yourselves on the back burner? Do you say you'll start tomorrow or you'll start next week? Don't put yourself last on the list: make yourself a priority. Decide to do it now, from today. Remember that we are responsible for ourselves: we must look after ourselves in order to feel better on all levels, physical, mental and emotional. We aim to achieve and maintain our health and wellbeing and want to feel happier. We want to live a productive life, live longer and be able to perform our duties and responsibilities independently. We also want to be around not only for ourselves, but for our friends, partners and families; so we can enjoy the experiences we want to have to the fullest.

Discipline

A good athlete can be seen at the end of the race not at the beginning. An old Greek saying

We need discipline if we are to achieve the necessary things we must do on a daily basis, to get to where we want. Just as an athlete needs to put in the training expected to produce the results they want. We need to do the work so we can see the results. We must keep a constant watch on our thoughts: keep that security guard at the door of our mind. We decide what we let into our mind. Those thoughts influence us and determine how we think and feel; they sway our decisions. Those thoughts, feelings and decisions determine our outcomes. Discipline is a necessity if we are to see results. So exercise your mental and physical discipline to do the acts needed to get the results you want.

It may sound easy in theory, but it requires daily awareness and vigilance to achieve results in any area of our life. It is up to us to be disciplined to do the work on ourselves, take the necessary actions and do the tasks needed to reach our goals. We must change our thoughts and our diet, do the exercise, and change our patterns and our feelings. We must discipline ourselves to take small steps daily, to build mental, emotional and physical strength. If we want to get from A to Z, we do it one step at a time. Get inspired, find a goal and ignite the light to motivate you to discipline yourself to achieve what you want. Being inspired and passionate makes it much easier to be disciplined to do things.

It takes discipline to get up in the morning, to do the exercise, to go to work and do everything we need to do. It takes discipline to do the things we have to do when we don't want to. It takes discipline to face the day when all you want to do is pull the covers over your head and go back to sleep. It takes discipline to put on a smile and a brave face when your world is falling apart, when you have lost a loved one, are facing bankruptcy or loss of a job, a terminal illness or misfortune. It takes discipline to get the necessary things we want in life. It takes discipline—but we must exercise discipline to heal ourselves and our lives. The more we exercise our discipline, the stronger we become. The stronger our bodies become, the healthier we feel and the better we look. The more we exercise discipline over our mind, the better we become at it and the quicker we get to being the way we want to feel and bring what we want into our world

For when we feel good, we feel happier. When we feel grateful we feel happier and we can attract what we want into our lives. We are vibrating at a higher level and so we attract more of the good things we want into our lives. When we feel sluggish and can't wake up and want to pull the covers over our heads, we don't have the energy, stamina or the will to focus our intentions. We don't have the motivation to do the exercise, or for all the demands that are required of us or to create and build our dreams. It's much harder to discipline ourselves and focus on being positive when our mind and body feels exhausted and depressed.

As mentioned, discipline is like a muscle, the more we use it the better we will get at it, and the stronger it will become. The more we practise this and discipline ourselves, the better we will be, the better we will feel, and the more we will attract what we desire into our life. Our spirit might say, 'yes', but our minds and bodies say, 'no way, I'm going back to bed today'. We need to look after our bodies, nourish them. Disassociate from the pressures of life and connect with who we really are. First and foremost we must focus and be grateful for this wonderful body that we have. Our body is magnificent and we need to respect it and look after it so it can function at its best capacity.

Small steps daily build on our disciplines. Every time we discipline ourselves, we become stronger emotionally, physically and spiritually. We will see the results if we do the necessary daily actions and disciplines. The more we exercise the more stamina our body will have and the better we will look and feel. The more we are disciplined to eat healthy foods, the better we will feel and look, the more energy we will have and the healthier we will be. The more we exercise our mental discipline to monitor and manage our thoughts by changing them when we are feeling negative to positive thoughts, the better we will become at it.

The person who can overcome their negative beliefs (demons) is on their way to heaven on earth. We need to develop a relationship with what we want and where we want to go or to bring into our life. It's the way we think and feel that determines what we attract.

Exercise

We need to exercise our bodies and our minds. Make a commitment that you are willing to stick to, whether it's a minimum 20 minutes a day, or 1 hour 3 to 7 times per week. You decide what results you want and how much time you commit to exercise—just get active. The more we exercise the better the results will be and the better we will feel. What goals do you have for your body? Work out a healthy weight for the body type you have and then work out how much time you must commit to exercise to achieve this. How will you achieve and maintain your health and exercise goals? Stretch your body daily or as often as you can. Take up tai-chi, yoga, or aerobics, walk, swim, ride your bike, play tennis or whatever sport you enjoy. Exercise and break into a sweat. Get active, get your heart rate up; the more you use your muscles, the stronger and more vital you are.

We need, too, to exercise our minds daily to be aware of what we are feeling and thinking consistently. If they are off track, we change the negative thoughts to positive thoughts and get back to where we should be. There will be challenging times, times when it is harder for you to be in charge of your thoughts—this is a given. We know that nothing is more important for us and our body than feeling good: we need to constantly check in on how we are feeling. Our emotions guide us, so we need to check in on our thoughts. If we find negative thoughts, we need to be vigilant in our attempts to weed them out and get back on track with good-feeling thoughts. We know that practice will lead to a faster return to good-feeling thoughts. Tai chi, pilates, karate and yoga are excellent forms of exercise for the body as well as the mind, and help to keep us centred and balanced. Meditation is an excellent mental discipline and exercise for our minds.

7

Integration

Balance

Balance is essential: a balance of work, rest, exercise and play—time for our creative outlets and for sharing our lives with family and friends. A balance of all things is good practice: do nothing to excess. Overworking ourselves and not letting our bodies rest and heal is not looking after ourselves. We must stop and smell the roses and be in the present as much as we can. Otherwise time just passes us by and we miss the beauty of life's experiences. Watch a sunrise, walk on the beach, walk in the rainforest, enjoy the beauty of a flower. The hug and innocence of a child and their outlook on life is priceless: revel in their joy, and let out your inner child. A good balance of foods and a good balance of work, rest and play make for a healthy body, a healthy mind and a happier you. If we push yourselves to the limit, make sure we take time out to recover, to rest, recuperate and re-energise. Always pushing yourself gives your body and mind no time to refresh and rejuvenate. Meditation balances our bodies and minds, and gets us into alignment with who we are, and away from the thought world. Sleep refreshes and repairs; the amount we require depends on the individual. Let your body guide you about how much it needs to feel good.

Simplify your life and get back to the basics of the previous eras. We only need to look at our society and our world, to realise that something is not right. Society is overflowing with crime, violence, drugs, divorce, debt troubles and illness. With all our technology and human advances, we have somehow become lost in the pressures of day-to-day living. Our goals of achieving more and more put us under more pressures and out of tune. We get lost in the mind and are missing the beautiful moment of now, wonder and oneness. We have forgotten to practise the teachings of the Bible. We must realise that we have to change the way we are doing things. We need to take away many of our pressures, and get back to the important things in life: love, family, giving, enjoying the now, being grateful for what we have, enjoying the abundance of Universe and its beauty. We must learn from the success of the older generations, of our ancestors, and combine them with the advances we have now. As we become more aware and more enlightened, we open the way for others to follow. This change will make a difference in our lives and our world, and the more people that change and awaken will change our society and eventually our Universe.

We all have the same divine intelligence within. It's not reserved just for some people; it's in all of us. When we awaken this power that lies within us all and let it guide our lives, we become co-creators. We love to create and bring into our reality what we want and desire: this helps us grow, change and evolve. When we do something well, we feel great satisfaction. The more experience we get the better and more confident we feel about ourselves. Wisdom only comes with life's experience, through experiencing the high and lows, life's happiness and heartaches, love and joy, light and beauty, darkness and pain. We learn from making mistakes, and from our success and victories. However, we must take the time to reflect, re-evaluate and learn from our mistakes and not keep on repeating them. Then we can reset our focus, our beliefs and create the new in order for us to move forward again. We have to use the lessons from our mistakes or failures if we are to get to the destination we desire, to grow and evolve.

Don't waste your emotions on regret; the past is the past, so move forward to the future. It's always natural to feel regret or sadness for mistakes, loss or bad decisions, but growth and healing lie in not dwelling and staying stuck on the regret. We saw earlier that acceptance and forgiveness are the keys to benefiting our future. The future is now and can be whatever it is you want it to be. We are only limited by our imagination, for what we can imagine and believe in our mind will come to pass. If we believe and can see ourselves fit and healthy, successful, wealthy, happy and peaceful—or whatever it is you desire—and if we truly desire it with all our being, it will be only a matter of time before it will come to us. We must have everything in moderation, nothing to excess; this applies to all things, food, work, play, rest and exercise. Balance is the key.

Patience

Patience is a virtue. Proverb

Learn to be patient, for your ideas need time to take shape and manifest. Enjoy the process of the idea or the project you are working on, whether it's a hobby, a piece of art a garden, a business, your health, a goal or a relationship. Don't wait till you get the thing you want before you are happy. If we wait to be happy only when we achieve things, our happiness will be short lived, for it won't be long before we want new desires—they are never ending. Be happy in the now, while you are expecting what you want to come. What you want will come to you in time; the Universe will deliver your desires if you desire them enough. When you can learn to have faith and believe the thing you desire will show up before it manifests—then you can enjoy the process of manifestation and expect its arrival.

Patiently sustain your desire and your belief and expect its arrival. It will show up in its own time. Trust that things will work out, and in the meantime enjoy the journey of creation. Rome wasn't built in a day. Everything of value takes time to build. Things built on a rock-solid foundation of absolute faith won't be blown away by the strong winds or storms of life. As mentioned, realise that it doesn't have to come in the time frame we think it should: it will come in its own time. When we believe, we develop a sense of expectancy; this allows the things we want to flow freely to us. It takes time to create anything substantial, be that a house, a garden, a piece of art, a business, a project, your goals, or healing yourself.

When our wings are damaged, we need time to heal and repair internally first. In time, our wings will repair themselves on the outside and we will be ready to come out of our cocoon and fly again. Accept what is now, hold onto faith, even when things seem hopeless and the pain seems too much to bear. When we accept what is, we can then go through the process of healing and allow the new to come in.

When the road you are standing on gives way and crumbles, it's as if your whole world caves in. One minute you are standing on solid ground and the next minute you're not. Everything is temporary, the good, the bad and the ugly. This too shall pass – it is now that we must be patient and resilient and hang on to hope for dear life, in order to move into the new and what we want to manifest.

Persistence

As Chinese wisdom teaches, the strongest steel is forged in the hottest fire, and the seeds of strength are often contained within the husk of weakness.

When we are down and broken and feel like we can't go on any longer, it is in the precise moment when we pick ourselves up off the ground, yet again, and decide to never give up. That is the beginning of our journey back to rebuilding and healing ourselves and becoming whole again. We don't need to know how we will do it: our vow and sheer will have already provided the spark needed to ignite the power within us.

Many people start with the positive affirmations, but because what they want is not coming to them, or in the time frame they want, they give up. It is especially crucial at this stage that we must persist and not give up. We must persevere, for, like a seed, it takes time for our desired thing to grow, to take hold and create new life. Our affirmations, attention, awareness and care will bring it about. We must put in the good soil and nutrients, then plant the seed, water it constantly and then it grows its own roots and starts to sprout. In time, its roots are strong enough to have a life of their own, but the plant still needs our attention, awareness and care. Things don't happen overnight, they take time. As every gardener knows, if they plant in spring, they will see their rewards in the summer. Sometimes it might take until the next year for the plant to flower, or even a few years to bear fruit. As every artist knows it takes time to create a great piece of art: it takes time, focus, persistence and patience.

As we grow and evolve, new ideas emerge and take shape; we connect with the piece we are creating and we become one with it. We give it life, it becomes a part of who we are as a person, and it's an expression of ourselves. A business usually takes three years before it starts to reap the rewards of the owner's efforts and hard work. A garden takes time before we are rewarded with fruit, vegetables or a beautiful display of flowers. We must do the hard work before we are rewarded for our efforts. We must persist and stick to our goals until we get them. Many people stop after a while because they don't receive what they want. Don't give up: it's a daily practice of disciplines that we must stick to if we are to achieve what we want. Remember sometimes it's not the smartest or most talented person who gets what they want: it's the one who holds onto their dreams and never gives up.

We must weather the storms of life no matter how severe. Some may be so unbearable and painful to endure. No matter how many times life knocks us over, we must find the courage and the will to get up and try again. The survivor's secret is not how many times we get knocked down, but how many times we get up.

It takes persistence and courage to get up in the morning, when we don't want to face the day and deal with anything, when things are going wrong and our world is crashing down and we feel shattered. But we still manage to soldier on and do what we have to do. When we put on a brave face; when all we want to do is run; when we face bankruptcy, divorce, a terminal illness or loss of career, or loss of something or someone we love, that's when we need persistence. It takes persistence to do all the things we need to do to get to where we want to go. It takes persistence to carry on being hopeful and positive. However we must decide to do everything it takes until we get to where we want. The inner steel within is forged by our iron will to push ahead and never gives up hope. Things are temporary—they don't stay the same forever. After loss, suffering or pain, healing and renewal come just as surely as the spring brings new growth. The old dies and fades away, to give way to the new, just as it does in nature.

When we are all out of faith and in a tunnel of darkness, we must hold on to that small ray of hope to pull us through misery, to find our way back to ecstasy again. Sometimes our greatest lessons come from losing, not from winning. When we lose our health, a loved one, our jobs, our money or all that we own, these things shape and define us and weave themselves into the tapestry of our souls. When we heal we become more; we go from broken to whole again and expand with the Universe and all that is. Don't lose faith in people, love or life's possibilities. We must put our faith in God and believe in life's wonderful possibilities, opportunities and that we will overcome anything that will come our way—no matter how many times we get knocked down. Don't lose hope for hope is like the sunshine to our soul. When it fades or dies, it must be ignited by us again. Make the choice to believe in life and its endless opportunities.

Never stray off your path

Never wander off your path. Every day we have to decide which road we take. What will be our actions and disciplines today? Are we going to focus on good-feeling thoughts, or are we just going to react to circumstances? Are we going to choose peace and harmony (aligning), or are we going to choose ego and conflict (resisting)? Are we going to do the actions necessary to bring in our goals?, or do we put it off till next week. Never stray off your path to the left or to the right, stay on your path, and stick to your goal. If we are committed to health, wellbeing and abundance; if we persist and stay on that road, we will get there. But we must be careful that we don't burn ourselves out. We decide how much work we want to put in—remember that slow and steady wins the race. We all know the story of the tortoise and the hare: it was the tortoise that won the race. Small steps daily all contribute to lasting success; they keep us on our path of commitment towards our goal. Small steps daily create mental, physical and emotional muscles and stamina.

We do the work on ourselves: we change our thoughts, we change our words, and we change our destiny. If we persist in our desire to get what we want, if we put in the work and do all the actions and disciplines necessary, we will get what we want in time. Things will come to us in their time, not our time. They will come to us when we stop resisting, when we open the door to them and allow them in. We need to create new positive patterns to replace our old negative resistant patterns.

Trust in your intuition (Infinite Intelligence, our Higher Power). We must listen to the small voice inside, our gut instinct: most people disregard it, and don't pay attention to it. The more we practise listening to it, the better and more aware we are, and the more we are aligning. When we are indecisive, that's the time to check in on how we feel and wait. When something doesn't feel right or feels bad, we are not on the right track; when something feels right, we're on the right track. How do we know for sure? Ask for signs; the more we practise awareness, the more in tune we will be, and the better we will become at it. People will always doubt, so they prefer to listen to the reasoning mind. But anyone who has ever achieved great success has trusted their intuition and followed the leads.

We all have goals we want to manifest; but remember it is the journey towards the goal that is the exciting part to enjoy, not just at the end when we get what we want. The leads or signs may come to you in a song or a book, from other people, or as a new idea. Be aware, observe, ask and we shall receive. Our job is to be a good receiver, to follow the leads, to take the necessary actions—then expect and prepare for our good to come to us.

Go forward and take the plunge. It takes more courage to have faith than it does to doubt and have fear. We must take the leap forward, even when we are scared or fearful.

Self-expression

Happiness. What happens to you does not matter, what you become through those experiences is all that is significant. This is the true meaning of life. Chinese wisdom

We each have a destiny that we alone are meant to fulfill. It is something we love to do and are drawn to. When we do it, time is forgotten, time stands still and we are totally immersed and absorbed in the moment. If we spent more time doing the things we love instead of on everything we have to do, we would feel a lot happier. Listen to that voice inside, follow our intuition and let it point us in the right direction. Most people doubt the still small voice. We have to be aware and open, and pay attention to any signs, and follow the leads. It might be music, gardening, law, or building or creating things. It might be a career or a hobby you want to pursue. It might be something we want to do for ourselves, or something for other people because we want to help them in some way. Whatever it is that we are drawn to and enjoy, the chances are that we'll be good at it. For when we love to do something we enjoy doing those things. Pay attention to what interests you and what you would love to do.

Choose to have peace in your life. Make nothing else more important to you than for you to feel good daily. If you can remember this as your daily ritual, you will have and maintain good health and wellbeing on all levels, physical, emotional and spiritual. Make it a conscious awareness to love yourself first: when we love and give to ourselves, we are respecting who we are. When we give to ourselves and take time out to rejuvenate and refresh our minds, bodies and souls, we are in a better place to be able to give to our family, friends, colleagues or anyone we meet. Give and receive love, experience life, be in the now moment as much as we can, otherwise life just passes us by. There is always so much to be done and not enough time, but we must make the time to care for ourselves. Let experiences touch us, for life is all about our experiences and how we feel.

The same event can happen to two people, but it's how each person feels about it that is their reality. So we can learn to look at things differently, from a different perspective, with a different set of lenses. Everybody has a different perception. As we change our perspective, and put on another pair of glasses, we see life from a totally different angle. We can see things in a broader view. It's as if our view to life has been uploaded to 360 degrees. Life is a gift: it is given to us for free. We must value, respect and look after our physical bodies, as well as our mind and our soul. This will allow us to have better experiences, have the energy to do things we want to do, and live a healthy, productive and long life. Sometimes we don't value things enough, or we don't realise how much we do have (especially when they are given to us for free). Sometimes we take things for granted and expect that things will always be the same. It's not until the things we do have are suddenly taken away from us that we realise how much we really do have.

Let things move us, touch us; experience life. Get in touch with our emotions, for they guide us. If we feel bad, we want to change the way we feel, so we can be in a good place to enjoy things. When we are not feeling well or are upset, we are so focused on what is wrong then we are absent from life, we are not in the moment. So we are actually missing out on the present, on our life which is a gift. Time passes and it can never be brought back again, so enjoy it all now to the fullest.

As we come to the end of this journey, I want to ask you some questions. It's up to you to answer these questions. If you haven't already done this, I hope you will take the time now to answer all the questions and to write down all the goals you want to manifest.

How will you take care of yourself today, tomorrow and the next couple of years? How will you take care of your body? What foods are you going to be committed to eating, and will you stick to following that diet? What actions do you have to start today and continue to take every day? Small steps daily make for a successful life and for bringing to you anything you want to achieve. What sort of relationships do you want to have? What goals do you have for the next year?

Where will you be 5 or 10 years from now? What do you want to bring into your life? What goals do you want to have achieved? What relationships will you have? What work do you want to be doing? What body do you want? How do you want your health to be?

You can create the life you want. You are the director and co-creator of your life.

Getting back to basics

In order for us to feel less pressured and anxious we must simplify our lives, take away as many of the stressors that you can, and then do what needs to be done. Do what you can, don't overdo things. What might have been all right for you ten years ago may not be as enjoyable for you now. Do we really need all the excess stuff that our society tells us we need and must have? If we only chase external things, we will never be happy for long. Look for things that make you feel happy and good within. When we do this we are on the road to real fulfillment, for fulfillment can come from the simplest things in life: walking on the beach, enjoying a sunrise, sharing a dinner or coffee with a friend; gardening, meditating and connecting to your source. It comes from giving your child a hug, or hearing them say they love you, looking at the beauty that abounds in this Universe, the flowers, the wildlife, and the countryside. We are blessed with abundant surroundings. But we need to slow down and take time to enjoy them. Time will pass us by, so enjoy the present moment, put on some music and let it resonate into your soul. Take a walk, ride your bike, or do some exercise.

Nourish your body with fresh healthy food, salads, vegetables and fruit. Technology is a wonderful thing, but we must remember to make more time for the other more important things in life. So turn off the technology and get outdoors. Pick up the phone and ring your friend. Talk to your partner and your family.

With our need for instant gratification, we have forgotten the basics and secrets of real happiness and fulfillment: by simplifying our lives, working on ourselves, finding solutions to our problems and working on our issues; fixing things when we need to, or when they are broken, rather than throwing them out and replacing them. Yet we must also recognise when it's time to get rid of or throw something out when it can't be fixed.

Learn from previous generations, and value the simplicity of their lives. As much as possible, accept that there is something terribly wrong with our society: increasing violence, sickness, cancers, divorce, debt, wars and poverty. They have always been there to an extent, but it is so prevalent now it has become an epidemic. As we combine the wonders of our generation with the basics of our ancestors, we can move forward to a greater way of being and living together in peace and harmony and healing for all of us.

We can decide to start right now: just be grateful and focus on all the good we do have. We have the greatest gift of all, the gift of life. Money can't buy what we have; it's ours for free. So let's respect ourselves and look after our minds and bodies and take responsibility for our lives. It's up to us to bring into our life all that we want. It's up to us to look after ourselves. Today is the first day of the rest of your life.

My message to you

I wish for you peace, health, wellbeing, wealth, happiness and abundance. We may never meet in person, but we have met here in the pages of this book in spirit and in the light. Go forward in faith, ignite your Power and make your life everything you want it to be, heal yourself and your life.

We can control our conditions by using these spiritual laws. Awaken the Trojan Warrior within you and link with Infinite Intelligence. We have been given this power and it is up to us to connect with it and use it in our lives. Let go and let God come into our lives (surrender your will). Let go of worry anxiety and fear, and replace them with trust, hope and faith. Ask and we shall receive, for God is the giver of gifts; we have to allow them in to receive them; become a receiver. We have been given a free will and we are the ones in charge of our thoughts, words, actions and reactions.

Feel the fear, take a leap of faith and do the things you want to do anyway.

Go forward, open the door to all your good and let it come in.

RESOURCES

Phoenix mythology
http://en.wikipedia.org/wiki/Phoenix_(mythology)
http://www.mythencyclopedia.com/Pa-Pr/Phoenix.
html#ixzz1HObpJrp6
http://www.ehow.com/about_6401530_phoenix-bird-information.
html#ixzz13cBS3cxU

Placebo
http://www.ehow.com/about_5074675_placebo-used.
html#ixzz13cUROKga
http://www.betterhealth.vic.gov.au/bhcv2/bhcarticles.nsf/pages/
Placebo_effect?open

Diet
http://www.natural-health-for-you.com/five-food-groups.html

Quotes   Scovel Shinn, Florence
          Or as referenced

The New King James Bible, New Testament, Thomas Nelson Inc. Nashville, Tennessee, 1979.
http://www.publicquotes.com
http://en.wikipedia.org

Bible texts
http://www.biblegateway.com
http://biblehub.com,com/john/8-7.htm
http://www.kingjamesbibleonline.org/Luke-19-10/

Books

Hay L, *The Power to Heal*, Hay House Australia, [Alexandria, 1985.

Hicks E and Hicks J, *The Amazing Power of Deliberate Intent*, Hay House Australia, Alexandria, 2006.

Hill N, *Think and Grow Rich*, Penguin Putnam Inc, Los Angeles, 2007.

Khamisa A and Quinn J, *Secrets of a Bullet Proof Spirit*, Allen & Unwin, Crows Nest, Australia 2009.

Robbins A, *Awaken the Giant Within*, Simon & Schuster, Sydney, Australia, 1992.

Rohn J, *5 Major Pieces to the Life Puzzle*, Brolger Publishing, Australia, 1994.

Tolle E, *The Power of Now*, New World Library, Hodder Australia, Sydney, 2004.

Williamson, M, The Age of Miracles, Embracing the New Midlife, Hay House Australia, 2008.

Cloud H Dr. Townsend J Dr. Boundaries When to say Yes when to say No To Take Control of Your Life, Zondevan Publishing House, Grand Rapids, Michigan, USA, 1992.

Scovel Shinn F. Wisdom of Florence Scovel Shinn, Simon & Shuster, USA, New York, 1989

Meditation CD

MacGregor, S. Acceptance, Healing Yourself, Peace

ACKNOWLEDGEMENTS

There are too many people to list separately, but you all know who you are.

Words won't do me justice and I will try not to leave anyone out.

To my gorgeous girls, Danielle and Christina, my rays of sunshine, you keep me going. I love you with all my heart. To my Mum and Dad, thank you for your love and support, your the best. Thank you so much to my brother Tony and his wife Simone for you support, love and prayers. To Phil and family, thank you for your support and prayers. To the doctors and nurses at Royal Brisbane Hospital and Princess Alexandra Hospital, words can't express my gratitude, and I will be forever grateful. My donor—thank you, my angel sent from heaven. I am forever indebted to you. The Leukaemia Foundation—thank you so very much for your help and support during my time of need, I am extremely grateful and humbled. To all of my wonderful relatives, I love you. Thank you for your love, wishes and prayers. My friends, old and new, you know who you are, I thank you all for your support and love. To Leon Nacson, thank you for your guidance, support and belief in me.

OVERVIEW

The story of a woman who achieved and lived the dream—the dream house, a multi-million-dollar property investment portfolio together with a beautiful family. Getting cancer was not part of the plan, yet life has its unexpected twists and turns.

This is the result of a survivor's personal journey and battle with leukaemia, major setbacks and challenges. She overcame cancer only to go through a separation from her sweetheart of 28 years. She reveals the secrets to healing ourselves from adversity and maintaining health and wellbeing, and bringing in what we want into our life.

Printed in the United States
By Bookmasters